Honey & Co.

Food From the Middle East

Sarit Packer &
Itamar Srulovich

Honey & Co.

Food
From
the
Middle
East

SALT · YARD
BOOK CO.

To my sabba Manny and my savta Cissie
I miss you every day – Sarit

———————

To my savta Esther and my sabba Yehiel
for all that was on and around your big table – Itamar

'I got hunger.' – Alice Russell

Contents

119

Fresh salads

139

Light Dinners

165

Balls & stuff

187

Slow cooked

263

Drinks

Welcome.

We are a couple. We met ten years ago in a restaurant kitchen in Israel, where we were both born. Sarit had just come back from London, having trained there as a chef and worked at the Orrery for two years, as part of the team that got them their Michelin star, working in the classic French brigade system, where hierarchy, discipline and meticulous cooking are the only way. These values clashed a bit with the hippy, happy, laissez-faire attitude of the Israeli cooking culture. Trying to get a bunch of Israeli know-it-all chefs to act like Swiss watchmakers was never going to work. I thought she was highly strung and uptight... We married a year later.

We were not an obvious match. I was a skinny 23-year-old beach bum. I thought I knew everything there was to know about cooking and food, but I always preferred sleeping or reading to working. She, a plump 24-year-old war machine with a Bolshevik work ethic and a spread-sheet for a brain, intent on a stellar career, had (still has) an endless interest in cooking and food, and a soft spot for beaches.

We spent a lot of time together at work and, by chance, we lived a couple of streets away from each other in Tel Aviv. We had a lot of mutual friends from the restaurant and we became close. Sarit would give me a ride to and from work in her decrepit Subaru. On Saturday morning she'd have to call me before she left the house to make sure I was awake for my shift. We would go to lunch together sometimes, or for a drink, and would bump into each other at the local video store (such things still existed back then).

Tel Aviv is a hot, sticky place from May till October. The only relief to be had from the heat of the eastern Med is on the beach, day or night. One such night, sweaty after slaving over a six-compartment pasta boiler and a 12-top gas range, we got in the car and decided to hit the beach on our way home. Six months later we moved in together.

The beginning was all about introducing each other to our favourite foods and places. I took my wife-to-be to Jerusalem, my home town, to Rochelle's Sandwiches – a hole-in-the-wall canteen where an ancient Tunisian woman and her daughter cooked the most delicious stews, soups and mezze; and to Philadelphia – a Jordanian restaurant in the old town of East Jerusalem where they serve such exotic dishes as pigeon stuffed with pine nut rice, and rabbit cooked in yogurt and raisins; and I made her try Jerusalem's best falafel, which she sneered at but secretly enjoyed.

In Tel Aviv I took her to Big Itzik, the best kebab shop in Jaffa, and told her how one day I would open the best kebab shop in the world; and we went to the Bulgarian grill by the beach, where we'd have aubergine salad and taramasalata and

kofta kebab seasoned with kashkaval cheese, and we would reek of garlic for days afterwards. Together we went looking for Eden, a famed Persian restaurant tucked in among the sex shops and brothels of Tel Aviv's red light district, that served the lightest, most fragrant chicken dumplings and herby stews.

When we went to her part of the world in northern Israel, she took me to Haifa's Wadi Nisnas market, where the finest vegetables and fruit in the land are to be had (all grown the old-fashioned way in someone's backyard, or field-foraged) and the most fragrant coffee is roasted and ground to order. She made me try Haifa's best falafel, which I sneered at but secretly enjoyed.

We went to the Turkish market to have oven-fresh *burek* and to buy *lakerda* (bonito cured in brine) from Turkey. She introduced me to the best hummus in Acre (which, I had to agree, is the best in the country) and, next door, the best seafood in the country – straight from the Acre bay day boats, which bring fish so fresh all it needs is a bit of salt and some charcoal smoke.

Our life then, as now, revolved around food. Through food we met and through it we got to know each other. Much has changed – the country, the climate, the things we eat and the people we eat them with – but food is a constant.

We came to live in London on Christmas Day 2004, because of an infatuation with a book: our favourite cookbook, *Nico*, by Nico Ladenis. It is full of fiery passion and precision cooking – with recipes that are still used in London's finest kitchens – and has the best introduction to a cookbook ever. It made London sound like the only place to cook. We came to London dreaming of high gastronomy and Michelin stars. We ended up at the Oxo Tower, cooking and overlooking our new hometown from the eighth-floor restaurant. We worked a lot and earned a little, and spent whatever we could on food. Eating out was Vietnamese or Spanish food, at landmark restaurants and new ones, upmarket or downmarket dim sum, and any kind of Indian. At home we would cook the food we craved: freshly chopped salad and tahini; lentil rice and lamb chops with cumin; chicken roasted with lemon and mint; eggs in fragrant, spicy tomato sauce; or fishcakes with tons of coriander and garlic.

After six years in various London kitchens I felt it was now-or-never time. I had always wanted us to open a place: a noisy, crazy, sexy, smoky, messy, food-/love-/ people-celebration of a place. My wife – sensible woman that she is – was very much against starting out on our own. She knew how much toil, heartache and trouble are involved in running a restaurant and she knew that the responsibility would all fall on her (it did), but I would hear nothing of it. My tutelage with the masterful Cornelia, my boss for the previous three years, had prepared me for whatever might come my way.

We wanted a neighbourhood place, somewhere that would create its own community, and as Sarit was busy setting up the ritzy NOPI in Soho, I started looking at abandoned shops on Coldharbour Lane in Brixton and the backstreets of Clapham North. I began planning menus, testing and costing dishes, cooking for everyone who wanted to eat (dinner at ours: some mezze to start, have a laugh, drink a beer, eat some more – a sizzling skewer, a slow-cooked stew – easy, tasty domestic comforts), trying to get a feel of what we wanted to do and how to do it. Working on financial projections; creating a playlist; choosing a font for a menu for a place that didn't exist – things that anyone with any grasp on reality would not have wasted time on. Fortunately, a grasp on reality is something I have never had, so I plodded along.

We viewed dozens of places; we made an offer on at least eight without any luck. Putting an offer on 25a Warren Street was a desperate act of faith in our imaginary restaurant. The street has a strong Eighties feel to it, and not in a hip, retro way. The place itself was tiny, coloured bright orange inside and out, with fluorescent green details, and had a persistent aroma of lasagne that still

today wafts out whenever someone turns on the air conditioning. But the room had nice proportions and a beautiful big glass front, plus there was an almost-functional kitchen of a decent size downstairs with a huge, beautifully made walk-in fridge. We had to admit that we were quite in love with the place despite all the cons. We told ourselves that if the Middle Eastern thing didn't catch on, we could always make a living selling lasagne and panini.

We were open for business six weeks after we signed the lease. We scoured eBay for bentwood chairs and kitchen equipment. I carried four chairs from Ealing to Brixton on the Tube; Sarit brought a heavy-duty industrial mixer from Croydon with the help of a big-hearted, broad-shouldered cabbie. Our only extravagance was the beautiful Moroccan tiles we got from a dealer whose showroom had burned down. We emptied our flat of kitchen equipment, cleaning equipment, in fact any equipment we could use, anything that would save us money. At our very first interview for front-of-house staff we fell head over heels in love with Rachael, just as everyone who meets her does.

We would start the day with a Turkish coffee and a vitamin drink. From 7am to 11am Sarit would bake the sweet things, I the savoury, then she would set up for lunch service and I would go upstairs. Working the front-of-house for the first time, I would manage simultaneously to

Welcome.

mess up the bookings, mess up the orders, mess up the waiters' station and mess up the till. Once a day I'd spill a drink on someone and would regularly be shouted at by Rachael, by Sarit, by angry customers... I loved (and still love) every minute of it. I also got to meet the people who made Honey & Co their own – the reason we opened the restaurant in the first place.

We did not know this part of the world at all. We thought most of our customers would come from the offices nearby. We didn't realise how residential the area is and, without being pompous, how much it needed a place like ours, and how lucky we were to land in this spot. We started attaching names to familiar faces: the beautiful blonde and her softly spoken husband were Rebecca and Matthew, from the gallery around the corner; the English father with the Spanish kids were Henry, Ivan and Lydia. Then we got to know some stories: Chrissie and Spencer live in LA half the time with Mr Love the cat and Shiksa the poodle, who we only ever saw in pictures; Deena is getting treated for cancer at UCH and, on the rare occasions she is hungry, rushes to us and orders half the menu, but only ever eats a little bit.

And more people came on board to help us. After a month of doing all the washing and cleaning ourselves, we hired Carlos, a sweet, funny Catalan who was the worst porter we've worked with. Giorgia di Marzo came to do the pastry, a feisty Italian

with an insatiable hunger for sweets and knowledge. Julia came to the savoury side, a Polish woman with an eastern soul and palate. And of course there was the Young family – Chelsea, Hayley, Ashleigh and Bonnie – a brood of tiny, perfectly formed sisters from South Africa with endless, tireless charm.

Our brainchild is now a reality – it is our day-to-day, our family and our job. It's hard, really hard. We work long, stressful hours and deal with the realities of pipes blocking, council officials visiting, staff getting ill, friends getting angry for being ignored and the constant fear of it all going wrong. But we are having more fun than we would ever have thought possible.

We wanted to write this book to capture the essence of who we are – not just the two of us but also our little restaurant and the hive it is, the people we work with, the people we feed and the customers who became friends, and the tasty, easy, homey food that brings us all together.

Itamar Srulovich
London, 2013

Basic instructions – the way we work

General preparation: Please read the entire recipe before you start cooking, or indeed shopping. Always good practice.

Weights: In some recipe lists I have stated the weight of prepared (i.e. peeled/ trimmed/ filleted/ picked) ingredients to give you a better idea of size – for example '1 red onion (about 100g)' – but don't get too hung up on this. If the peeled onion weighs 20g more than stated, don't discard the extra; it won't ruin your dish, and my mum taught me never to waste food. The weights are there as guidance.

Cooking and baking temperatures: I do most of my baking and roasting in a fan-assisted oven, as it is faster and has a better heat distribution than a convection oven. I have given other oven settings (for gas and convection) throughout, but you will still have to use your discretion as regards your own oven – which may cook hotter or cooler than the dial says – and how it affects cooking times. I have tried to give you a description in each recipe of what the end result should look like, to help you gauge when things are ready.

Water: On the subject of weights, I often weigh the water for recipes rather than measuring it in a jug, as weighing tends to be more accurate. If you'd like to do the same, it's a very easy conversion to make, as 1ml water = 1g water.

Cream: Similarly, although I have given cream measurements in ml for convenience, I tend to weigh it when cooking, for better accuracy. While cream is slightly more dense than water, the difference is so small that you can still use a 1ml = 1g conversion without any problems with the recipes.

Sugar and salt: When we say sugar, we mean caster sugar unless otherwise specified; and salt means table salt unless otherwise stated. We use Maldon sea salt to finish dishes, rather than to cook with, unless the recipe specifically calls for sea salt as an ingredient.

Garlic: We always use fresh garlic and not pre-minced, as the flavour changes when it has been sitting around for too long.

Lemon juice: We use freshly squeezed lemon juice for the same reason.

Flat bread: The Middle Eastern way is to always have pitta or some other flat bread at the table, to soak up juices and add substance. You don't have to, but it helps.

Nuts, raw and roasted:

We use a lot of nuts in our food and the recipe will always state whether they should be roasted or not. If you are roasting them, the best way is to lay them on a baking tray and roast them in the centre of the oven at the temperature and for the time set out in the table below. They should go golden (or, in the case of pistachios, greeny-golden) – if they have the skin on and you are not sure, split one in half to check whether it is a light golden colour. Don't let the nuts brown unless the recipe requires it, as they will become bitter, and do remember that they will continue to roast on the hot tray, so if you think you left them in the oven a little too long, quickly transfer them to a cold bowl to stop them cooking any further. You can also roast nuts on the stove in a dry frying pan on a very low heat, shaking the pan every few seconds. This requires more attention, but far less electricity, than oven-roasting. Don't roast more than you need (apart from the ones you intend nibbling on), as the flavour is best when the nuts are freshly roasted.

Roasting times and temperature for nuts:

Here is a quick guide to the main nuts we use and some recommendations for flavoured nuts to nibble with your drinks.

Nut	Temperature	Time	Possible additions
Almonds, skin on	180°C/160°C fan/ gas mark 4 (nice and low to roast through without burning)	15–18 minutes	Olive oil and salt
Pine nuts	200°C/180°C fan/gas mark 6	5 minutes, shake the tray, then a further 5–8 minutes till golden	
Pistachios	200°C/180°C fan/gas mark 6	10–12 minutes	Olive oil, salt and some lemon zest
Walnuts	200°C/180°C fan/gas mark 6	10 minutes	
Hazelnuts (skinless)	180°C/160°C fan/ gas mark 4 (nice and low to roast through without burning)	14–16 minutes	Tiny drizzle of honey and some chilli flakes
Cashew nuts	190°C/170°C fan/ gas mark 5	8 minutes, shake the tray, then a further 8 minutes till golden	1 egg white and 1 tbsp ras el hanut spice mix for every 500g of nuts

Spices:

- We try to grind our own spices wherever possible, the only exceptions being ground turmeric, ginger, pimento (allspice) and cinnamon, which are all hard to grind on your own. We love using a small coffee grinder, but a pestle and mortar is really good too and makes you feel as if you've worked for your flavour. Avoid buying pre-ground spices if you can, or make sure to buy from a shop with a high turnover so that they are as fresh as possible.

- When preparing ground cardamom, I grind the whole pods as I find that this gives the best flavour.

- We also use a lot of cinnamon sticks in our cooking. They are interchangeable with cassia bark, which I actually prefer as it imparts a mild hint rather than a strong hit. If you are using very thick, tightly-rolled cinnamon quills, use half the amount in the recipe. Don't replace with ground cinnamon.

- Chilli is an issue for us. I am not a huge fan. I like a tiny note of spice that brings out the flavour; Itamar loves spicy, hot food, and enjoys the sensation of little beads of sweat forming on his nose when he eats. The amounts given in the recipes are my preferences. I recommend you start with these as you can always add more; it is harder to reduce the chilli-hit once it is in. The heat will also greatly depend on the type of chilli being used and the season – in general terms, the larger the chilli, the milder it is; and in summer I find that they get an extra kick from the sun and are spicier. Removing the seeds and white membrane reduces the heat if you want to take it down a notch. The best way to decide how much to use is to cut a tiny piece off the end of the chilli and taste it: if it kicks you in the mouth, take it easy.

A note on quantities:

The first part of our book is dedicated to mezze, the traditional way to start a meal in the Middle East. You can offer as much or as little variety as you wish, from a couple of dishes to a whole tableful. Obviously this makes it hard to give accurate guidance as to how many people each recipe will feed, as it depends how many other mezze are being served at the same time. Most recipes give an estimated portion yield, but do take into account that if you are serving eight guests with eight varieties of mezze, you will not need to double the recipes even if they say 'serves 4', as your guests will only need a bite of each. It takes a little practice to figure the perfect amount of mezze for a starter – you need to make sure that everyone will still have enough room for the main course, so aim to serve portions on small plates with just enough to allow everyone to try some but not to overeat. The same logic applies for the mains – if you are making more than one dish you can cut down on quantities for both. That said, no one ever died from having nice leftovers...

Base recipes

Here are a few recipes for ingredients we use regularly, and which form the basis of our food. Try to find the energy to make the spice mixes at least once. You will not regret it.

Sweet spice mix

We use this mostly for cakes and baked goods, and also for preparations that require a lighter touch.

10 cardamom pods
6 cloves
½ nutmeg
1 tsp whole fennel seeds
2 tsp whole mahleb seeds
3 tsp ground ginger
4 tsp ground cinnamon

Preheat your oven to 190°C/170°C fan/ gas mark 5. Roast the cardamom pods, cloves and nutmeg on a baking tray for 5 minutes, then add the fennel and *mahleb* seeds and roast for another 5 minutes. Remove from the oven and allow to cool completely before grinding and then mixing with the pre-ground ginger and cinnamon. Store in an airtight container. This will keep for up to 6 months, but I always think you should try to use it within 2 months to get the flavour at its best.

Baharat – savoury spice mix (aka 'Sarit spice' at Honey & Co)

This, like its namesake in our kitchen, is the backbone of everything we make and, like its namesake, has endless depth and beauty, and improves almost anything. You can use ready-made *baharat* spice mix instead, or Lebanese Seven Spice mix, which is sold in most large supermarkets – it will taste slightly different but will still be tasty.

1 dried chilli
3 tsp coriander seeds
4 tsp cumin seeds
2 tsp ground pimento (allspice)
1 tsp white pepper
½ tsp ground turmeric
2 tsp sweet spice mix (see above)

Preheat your oven to 190°C/170°C fan/ gas mark 5. Crack the dried chilli open and shake out the seeds. Place the deseeded chilli on a baking tray with the coriander and cumin seeds and roast for 6 minutes. Remove from the oven and allow to cool entirely on the tray. Crumble the chilli between your fingers, then grind all the roasted spices to a powder. Mix with the dried ground spices and store in an airtight container. It will keep for up to 6 months, but ideally use within 2 months for the full effect.

Preserved lemons – two ways (whole and sliced)

Preserving whole lemons is a slow process and you won't see any results for at least 6 weeks, but it is worth it. If you need preserved lemons more speedily than this, you can buy them ready to use from many delis, but for a quick home-made fix, follow our preserved lemon slice recipe instead.

To sterilise a jar for the lemons, preheat the oven to 200°C/180°C fan/gas mark 6. Wash the jar (and its lid) in hot soapy water. Rinse well and dry thoroughly with a clean tea towel. Place on a baking tray and heat in the oven for 5 minutes. Alternatively pour boiling water into the clean jar, count to ten, then pour the water out and fill the jar immediately.

Whole preserved lemons

This is not so much a recipe as a preparation guide – you can preserve as many lemons as you want or think you will use. Make these when good small lemons are in season and going for a good price. Try to buy unwaxed ones, but otherwise wash the lemons well with soapy water to remove as much wax as possible before you start.

Use a small knife to score a cross three-quarters of the way down into each lemon so it opens up like a flower but stays intact. Fill the cut space with loads of sea salt and put the lemons in a sterilised jar, pushing as many as you can into the jar. Seal the jar and leave it on the windowsill for 2 weeks.

Liquid will start to come out of the lemons and should reach about halfway up the jar by the end of the fortnight. Open the jar and push everything down with a spoon (not your hands), then cover the lemons with olive oil and seal the jar again. Leave to rest in a dark place for at least a month before use. Once opened, these will keep for about a month at room temperature, or up to 3 months if you store them in the fridge.

Preserved lemons are used for cooking, rather than as a condiment or garnish. When you require one, you will need to pull it out carefully, using a pair of tongs or a fork (not your hands, so as not to contaminate the rest of the batch). Cut it open to remove the inner flesh and pips – discard these and use the lemon skin only for the recipe.

Preserved lemon slices

4 small unwaxed lemons
3 tbsp salt
1 tsp chilli flakes
enough olive oil to cover

Halve the lemons and slice as thinly
as you can – you can use a food processor
blade or a mandolin. Remove any pips
you come across. Place the slices in a
bowl and sprinkle with the salt and chilli
flakes. Allow to sit for 30 minutes at
room temperature.

Mix again, then push the lemon slices into
a sterilised jar so that they are tightly
packed with all the liquid that accumulated
in the bowl. Cover with olive oil and seal
the jar. These will be ready to use the next
day, but will improve with time. Once
opened, store in the fridge and use within
a month.

When you come to cook with them, just
take as much as you need for the recipe.
Chop and use the entire slice – you don't
have to discard the flesh as you do for
whole preserved lemons. The slices can
be eaten as a relish with fish or chicken
dishes, and you also use them mixed with
mayonnaise and harissa to accompany a
great chicken or tuna sandwich.

Tahini

The quality of your tahini depends hugely on the type of tahini paste you use. We use Al-Yaman from Lebanon which is delicious, but if you are lucky enough to find any of the Palestinian varieties, especially the Prince and Dove brands, you are in for a treat. The best tahini we've ever had is Altan Manisalı from Turkey – it is available from Namlı, the wonderful deli in the Egyptian market in Istanbul, if you are ever in the area. As a rule you are looking for something from Lebanon, Palestine or Turkey. We didn't like the Greek tahini we tried, nor the health-food shop variants. Avoid whole or black sesame tahini. We make our tahini in a food processor, as it gives a smooth, airy, mousse-like texture, but you can achieve good results with a bowl, a spoon and some wrist action.

Will yield about 240g

125g tahini paste
1 clove of garlic, peeled and minced
a pinch of salt, plus more to taste
juice of 1 lemon, plus more to taste
about 120ml water

Place the tahini, minced garlic, salt and lemon juice in a bowl or food processor, add half the water and mix. It will go thick and pasty but don't fear – just continue adding water while mixing until it loosens up to a creamy texture. Don't be tempted to add too much water as the mixture will go runny, but if this happens, you can always bring it back with a little extra tahini paste. Taste and adjust the salt and lemon to suit your taste buds. You can keep tahini in an airtight container in the fridge for 2–3 days, but it will thicken and the flavour may need adjusting with a little more salt and/or lemon. As a result we think it is best to make it and eat it the same day – fresh is best.

Zehug

This delicious preparation is at the heart of Yemeni cooking and eating – Yemenis travelling abroad have been known to take a jar with them, as food is not considered palatable without it. Traditionally it is pounded to a paste on a special grinding stone. Alternatively, if you prepare industrial quantities as some families do, a meat grinder works well. You can use a food processor to produce good results too, but it's worth making this with a pestle and mortar at least once, as it's very satisfying.

Will yield about 200g

2 bunches of coriander, washed well
1 green chilli
2 cloves of garlic
a pinch of salt
½ tsp ground cardamom pods (page 11)
1 small tomato, diced
2 tbsp olive oil

Grind all the ingredients apart from the olive oil together to form a thick, textured paste. Then use a spoon to stir in 1 tablespoon of olive oil. Scoop the paste into a small jar and top with the second tablespoon of olive oil – this will help preserve the green colour and stop the paste oxidising. Use within a week. Try it on all your food; it will add a touch of spice to every dish.

Everything

So named because we use it on everything. It is always in our kitchen. This simple condiment is traditionally served with hummus, vibrant against the creamy comfort of the dip, and though it is a mix of some very potent ingredients, they somehow balance each other to create a very mellow, interesting result. Sweet and sour, hot and earthy, it has everything you need. It works with so many things from salads to steak, and is wonderful on simply-roasted fish. Remove the seeds from the chillies for a very mild result, or leave them in if you like a bit more bite.

*3 cloves of garlic, peeled and finely chopped
    or crushed
½ small red chilli, very finely chopped
½ small green chilli, very finely chopped
¼ tsp ground cumin
¼ tsp salt
1 tsp honey
juice of 1 lemon*

Mix all the ingredients together in a bowl and leave for 10 minutes or so. The lemon will 'cook' the chilli and garlic a bit, the honey rounds the flavour and the cumin grounds it. This will keep for 2–3 days if stored in an airtight container in the fridge, but the flavour will mellow the longer you keep it.

Meshwiya & matbucha

Worth mentioning here are *meshwiya* and *matbucha*, meaning 'roasted' and 'cooked' in Arabic. They are two preparations made with the same ingredients, more or less, but one is roasted and one cooked (as it says on the tin). Their recipes are tied to specific dishes in this book – check out octopus in *meshwiya* sauce (page 200) and *matbucha* (page 77) – but in the restaurant we use them for pretty much everything, as should you.

Mezze.

A Moroccan family that adopted me for a while would start their Friday feast with a bowl of fried green chillies, bread and salt. You would peel the papery skin off the chilli, sprinkle with salt and down it in one. The pain from the heat would make you sweat and feel like your ears were about to pop, then you'd have some bread and go for more. Hard to explain why but hard to stop. Chilli heat is meant to build your appetite, and you'd need a big appetite for the feast that would follow – the combination of Moroccan generosity and Jewish anxiety meant that the Friday night dinners in this house were an epic feat, a culmination of days of shopping and cooking, generations of experience and the labour of many hands.

After the chillies, the table would fill up with so many different plates. *Kemia*, the North African term for mezze or starter, would be olives and pickles and mounds of bread, and purées of fava and pumpkin to dip it in, and salads, cooked or raw – some were weekly staples, some so specifically seasonal and obscure they were made only once a year, if that. Most of us around the table worked in restaurants and hotels, and worked really hard. The *kemia* for us was not only the beginning of the meal but the end of a hard week's labour, and the beginning of weekend fun time – not that you could manage much by the end of the meal. After the salads was soup; after that fish – a whole one per person; after that would be couscous, naturally, with chicken or lamb but really you should have a bit of both; and then a green salad, a legacy from the French. Dessert would be little cakes in rose syrup, savoury biscuits with fennel seeds, fruit and fresh mint tea in front of the TV. You really don't want to eat so much but when everything is so good, you can't help it.

It is such a nice way to start a meal – a table laden with little things to nibble, their beauty and quality a sign that good things are happening in the kitchen and are coming your way. In the restaurant we offer a selection of five mezze for lunch and up to ten for dinner, but at home we usually keep things very simple – good olives, good bread and a good something to dip your bread in. Pickles are always nice for crunch and colour, but fresh radishes, carrots or kohlrabi are just as nice. This is enough – anything else you care to prepare is a wonderful treat: fresh fish cured quickly, something hot and cheesy from the oven, crisp and spicy from the pan... the more the merrier, although it's nice to keep it to one or two bites of each, to leave some room for what's coming next.

Raw &
Cured.

We were driving north to the old coastal town of Acre – a beautiful maze of cobbled streets, elegant mosques in their pillared courtyards, arched doorways of Templar churches, all wrapped up in a wall fortified through centuries of fear of marauding fleets, which periodically came charging from the pretty Mediterranean bay beyond.

We came from quite a different place: the sooty, sweaty streets of Tel Aviv, where we lived at the time, a very sad and stressful period for us. I had just stormed out of a job that I loved, ripping ties with friends who were like family, and started a job which I hated. Sarit had just walked out of a business she had set up, leaving when it turned from a boutique bakery to a cookie factory, breaking her heart on the way; she too was in a job she knew was going nowhere. We had been living together for a year then and were very much in love, but we both realised that something had to give. So we drove to Acre for some fun. Cobbled streets and mosques and bays are all fine, but we of course went to eat: this particular bay happens to bring ashore some of the best seafood you can find any-where, and nowhere does this produce get treated better than in one restaurant in a parking lot overlooking the bay.

At this restaurant they gave us cold white wine that had been made nearby, fresh bread and olives, sweet aubergines steamed and marinated, fresh anchovies that they cured themselves and raw local prawns that were sliced thinly and seasoned gently with a few rounds of chilli, some sea salt and olive oil.

At this restaurant we realised how far we were from where we wanted to be, and how much we needed a change. It was there that we decided to up camp and go travelling abroad, and where I finally managed, by the by, to convince Sarit to marry me – not least because I needed a UK work visa. I had asked a few times before but she'd never seen a reason to agree.

The trip back to our flat had a different feel altogether. 'I have a new lease on happiness,' she said to me, which is one of the nicest things you can hear anyone say, doubly so when it's someone as reserved and frosty as Sarit.

The rest of 2004 was just as turbulent, full of highs and lows – Sarit was diagnosed with a medical condition that cast a big shadow over our travel plans, and a rift started that year between my family and me that would eventually tear my relationship with them apart for a long time to come. But that was also the year we got married and so the best year of my life, and at the very end of that year, on 23 December, we landed at Heathrow with our clothes and duvet, and a new lease on happiness.

Uri buri prawns

Try this when you get your hands on fresh, good-looking prawns – small ones work best: about the size of your little finger. It'll make for a very pure and flavoursome mouthful, and may give you a new lease on happiness.

Serves 4 (allow 2–3 prawns per person)

8–12 fresh prawns (depending on size)
1 red chilli
sea salt
1 lemon
the best olive oil you can find

Peel and de-head the prawns. Lay each one on its side on the chopping board, slit along the back, remove the brown intestine line and then slice it down the middle lengthways, opening it into two halves. Spread all the prawn halves flat on a serving plate, cut surfaces facing up, and pat them down a little with your fingers to flatten.

Cut the chilli into rings, as thinly as you can, and place a slice on each piece of prawn (you won't need to use the entire chilli). Season with a little sea salt and then squeeze the juice of the lemon all over the plate and drizzle with the olive oil. Allow to sit for 5 minutes, then close your eyes, imagine the sea and eat.

Lamb kubbe nia

Kubbe nia can be seen as the Middle Eastern answer to steak tartare – the finest meat chopped finely and seasoned with all kinds of piquant goodness. Bulgar wheat is a traditional accompaniment, and we like to add a bit of tahini to the mix to bind it all together.

Makes 14–16 small balls

2 tbsp bulgar wheat
a pinch of salt
2 tbsp boiling water
150g lamb loin fillet
½ onion, peeled (about 50g)
1 small clove of garlic, peeled
1 small green chilli, deseeded
1 small bunch of coriander, chopped (3 tbsp)
¼ tsp sea salt
a pinch of white pepper
1 tbsp tahini paste
juice of ½–1 lemon (to taste)

Start by mixing the bulgar wheat, salt and boiling water, cover and leave for 5 minutes.

Chop the lamb, onion, garlic and chilli as small as you can, but don't use a food processor as it will affect the texture, and this is the whole point of this dish. Combine with the remaining ingredients and mix well. Form into small balls about the size of a whole walnut and serve.

You can lay them on a bed of lettuce so that your guests can lift a small piece of lettuce with the meat inside.

Sea bream kubbe nia

This is a fish version of the lamb dish above. It is fresh and moreish and we love to serve it in Little Gem lettuce boats as a kind of posh canapé, but you can also create little balls if you prefer.

Will fill 10–12 Little Gem lettuce boats

2 tbsp bulgar wheat
a pinch of salt
3 tbsp boiling water
1 sea bream, filleted and skinned
  (ask your fishmonger to do it)
4 sprigs of mint, picked and chopped
2 spring onions, chopped (green and
  white parts)
½–1 green chilli, deseeded and chopped
juice of ½ lemon (1 tbsp)
1 tbsp olive oil
10–12 Little Gem lettuce leaves

Start by mixing the bulgar wheat, salt and boiling water, cover and leave for 5 minutes.

Dice the bream into small cubes. Mix in all the other ingredients, but just use half the chilli to start with and taste the mixture before deciding whether you want to add the remaining half.

Place a spoonful of the mixture in each lettuce leaf and set together on a serving plate. You may want to serve some additional lemon wedges on the side.

Sardines cured in vine leaves

This is useful and cost-effective party food – make it when you have a crowd coming, and hold some back for post-party nosh. Fresh sardines give you that saline sea-flavoured hit normally associated with more upmarket foodstuffs like oysters or caviar. Cured like it is here, this cheap ingredient is better than both, I think, and makes for a truly luxurious eat.

4–6 sardines (up to 100g each),
    filleted and trimmed
10–12 vine leaves in brine (the ones
    you get from a jar or vacuum-packed)
½ lemon
2–3 tsp sea salt
60–100ml olive oil

Start by removing the thin membrane that coats the skin of the fish – you can do this easily by scraping at the tip of the fillet with a sharp knife to expose the membrane, then grabbing it with your fingers and pulling. Repeat with the rest of the fillets.

Use half the vine leaves to line a wide colander or a cooling rack on a tray. Slice the lemon into thin slices and lay them on the vine leaves.

Next, lay the fillets skin-side down on the leaves and sprinkle with the salt, so every fillet gets a light sprinkling all over. It is time to put the sardines to bed – cover them with the remaining vine leaves and pat them down with your fingers so the vine leaves cling to the fish and they are snugly tucked in. Allow to sit like this for 15 minutes. They will have exuded some liquid, so pat them down again and leave for another 15 minutes.

When the time is up, remove the top layer of leaves (you can use these to garnish your serving plate if you want) and, using some kitchen paper or a clean cloth, pat the sardines to dry them and remove any excess salt. Pack them tightly (like sardines) into a small container, discarding the bottom layer of leaves and lemon slices, then pour over the olive oil (enough to cover them) and seal until you come to serve.

The sardines will be ready to eat in 20 minutes, and will keep well in the fridge for 2–3 days.

Serving suggestions for the cured sardines:

Tomato seeds, sour cream and spring onion
When you are ready to serve, lay the sardines on a plate. Halve a tomato and squeeze it over the plate as you'd squeeze a lemon, so all the seeds and juice come out and add freshness and zing. Serve with a small tub of sour cream and 2 finely chopped spring onions. A loaf of the potato bread on page 61 would be a great addition, or you could buy a crusty loaf.

Roasted pepper and olives on toast
Cut the sardines into small bite-sized pieces. Use the roasted pepper recipe from page 43 and halve a few black olives of your choice (we always favour the juicy Kalamata olives). Stack them all onto toasted bread (the Bukhari on page 58 would work best, if you wanted to make it) and add some chopped parsley or thyme.

Hard-boiled egg, capers and harissa paste
Boil some nice eggs (you can buy great eggs in supermarkets – we favour Burford Brown or Cotswold Legbar eggs, as they have amazing yolks and a great flavour). Give them 3 minutes boiling in salted water, then allow to cool in the water for 5 minutes before peeling. Grate the eggs on the rough grater and serve with capers and harissa paste on the side for people to help themselves.

Mackerel cured in oil

Autumn brings an abundance of bonito to the eastern Mediterranean. To make the most of that glut, they cure them to make *lakerda* – a Balkan delicacy – served on little plates with chopped onion and booze, or on bread with cucumber for lunch. This dish is not *lakerda* but it hits the same buttons. In England bonito is available all year round: caught in and imported from the northern Atlantic, it is fattier, a bit bland and very expensive. Much better to use mackerel, the pauper-prince of the British catch.

Using 200g of filleted fish or a whole mackerel of 350–400g which will yield approximately 200g of fillet, this makes a nice starter for 2 or serves 4 as a mezze

1 lovely fresh mackerel, filleted (net weight 200g)
½ tsp whole yellow mustard seeds
½ tsp whole peppercorns
1 tsp sea salt
1 garlic clove, unpeeled
2 strips of lemon skin (peeled off with a peeler)
1 dried chilli – shake out the seeds
2 bay leaves
olive oil to cover (about 180ml)

Place the fish, skin-side down, in a small frying pan that can contain it snugly – cut the fillets in half if that makes it easier. Then sprinkle with the mustard seeds, peppercorns and salt, and place the garlic clove (whole), lemon peel, chilli and bay leaves on top. Cover with the oil and set on a very low heat to slowly warm the oil. Once bubbles start to form, cover the pan with a lid and turn the heat off – the fish will continue to cook in the residual heat. It will take about 15 minutes if you want to use it straight away, or you can just leave it until the oil has cooled down, then store in an airtight container in the fridge until ready to use. It will keep for a week or so.

Serving suggestions for the cured mackerel:

With baby potatoes and mint

Boil baby potatoes in lots of salted water (we use 1 teaspoon of salt for every litre of water) until they are soft. Strain them and, with the back of a wooden spoon, crush them a little. Add 3 tablespoons of the curing oil and the leaves from a small bunch of mint, and mix around while still hot to infuse the flavour. Then flake the fish over and serve.

Tunisian-style toasties

Cook some eggs, peel and cut into wedges. Slice a crusty loaf or baguette into thick slices, brush each piece with a little of the curing oil and toast until golden. Flake the fish on top and add a dollop of harissa paste and a thin slice of preserved lemon (page 15).

With celery, parsley and cherry tomatoes

Pick loads of parsley leaves, cut thin slices of celery and shallots or red onion if you want. Add the mackerel flakes, dress with some lemon juice and oil from the curing. You can add some halved cherry tomatoes for juiciness.

Cured sea bream with pomegranate juice & cumin

Julia was a good friend and a customer before she came to work with us. She has uncompromising good taste and an interesting opinion about everything. She had this dish one night for dinner, and copious amounts of wine, and asked if she could come and work with us. We were thrilled of course, and just hoped she wouldn't sober up and change her mind. She hasn't yet. She now runs our kitchen with efficiency and grace, sharing her curiosity and love of good food.

1 sea bream, filleted and skinned
(ask your fishmonger to do it)
1 green chilli, deseeded
½ lemon
2–3 sprigs of fresh oregano
sea salt

For the dressing
1 pomegranate
2 tbsp olive oil
½ tsp ground cumin
½ tsp sea salt

A 500g fish will be enough for 4–6 people as a mezze

Cut the pomegranate in half and squeeze one half over a bowl to produce 2–3 tablespoons of juice (it is easier than it seems), then pick some seeds out of the other half to use as garnish later on. Mix the juice with the olive oil, cumin and salt.

Slice the green chilli very finely and place a sliver on every slice of fish. Squeeze the half lemon all over the plate, then pour over the dressing, making sure all the fish gets some. Sprinkle on the picked oregano leaves and a touch of sea salt. Allow 5 minutes for the flavours to combine, then garnish with the reserved pomegranate seeds and serve.

Place the skinless fillets on a clean board. Slice them as thinly as you can and lay them flat on a large serving plate. Try to keep all the pieces in a single layer so they all get seasoned.

Raw & Cured.

Fresh vegetable mezze

We always like to serve some form of fresh, cooked or raw vegetable at the start of a meal, when we get something nice. We may add some salt or a dipping sauce. Here are some of our favourites:

Little radishes with paprika salt
Quarter or halve the radishes and place them in a bowl of cold water. Mix 1 tablespoon of sea salt with half a teaspoon of smoky paprika. Remove the radishes from the water just before serving and either sprinkle with the paprika-salt or serve it on the side.

Shaved fennel with lemon and oil
Cut the fennel into thin strips. Squeeze over the juice of a lemon and add a tablespoon of olive oil and a pinch of salt.

Kohlrabi with chive sour cream
Peel the kohlrabi and cut into wedges. Serve with a little dish of chive sour cream (page 96) or good, thick yogurt.

Corn with chilli flakes
Boil the corn in water seasoned with 1 teaspoon of salt, 1 teaspoon of sugar and a pinch of turmeric for every litre, as this adds a great sweetness and intensifies the natural flavour. Drizzle with olive oil and chilli flakes.

Canned & Pickled.

Three weeks after we signed the lease on 25a Warren Street, we had done all we could afford to do, which was not much. The shop we took over had good bones and a good enough figure, but it was painted a bright fluorescent orange colour inside and out, like an overflow of spray tan from the tanning shop next door, and had crusty laminate floors. It had a good functioning kitchen with almost all the equipment we needed and a surprisingly big cool room in the middle, the cold heart of the place. The bathroom was a funny shed in a tiny patio area (it still is).

The refit was done on a shoestring budget. We saved wherever we could, begging for discounts and haggling hard, trawling the Web for second-hand items and job lots, meeting shady characters in London's outskirts. The only extravagance we allowed ourselves was the blue Moroccan tiles we got for the dining-room floor. We saw them first online and fell in love. We went to see them in a showroom in Vaux-hall, only to discover it had burned down. Further investigation led to an afternoon rendezvous on an industrial estate in World's End (only in London could this be an actual place name) with a middle-aged hippy called Michael, who has a workshop in Morocco and could get them done for us in two weeks. We ordered them after haggling as much as we could, saved the guy's number in our phones as 'Michael Tiles', shook hands and hoped for the best.

During the two weeks' wait we had to get everything else done. We hired a team of accident-prone Poles to eradicate every trace of orange from the walls and shop-front, and to get the floor ready for the arrival of our Moroccan beauties. Calls to Michael Tiles to check on their progress proved futile, as he would not answer and would not return messages, a fact that made us very nervous and also doubt the wisdom of doing deals on a traffic island under a plum tree, without any paper trail or witness. But they did come, three days early and without warning; a truck just dropped an unlabelled pallet on the pavement by 25a Warren Street, much to the perplexity of our builders. The tiles were tightly nestled in their boxes, still wet from the workshop, smelling a bit old-timey and third-worldly, and beautiful.

Two days later they were laid and treated (one made its way home to be used as a mouse pad and a pot stand), the first veg delivery arrived, along with a bank statement that showed how little was left of our life savings, and the panic that such things bring ensued. We entered our kitchen to cook for the first time, and the first thing we did was preserve lemons – bright yellow jars to place on our shelves, to complement the colour and origin of our tiles, to perfume and flavour our food, and to place our hope in a fortunate future.

A newish tradition is to use cola bottles for pickling; their narrow tops echo the shapes of the clay pots that were used in the old days. Cucumbers the size of your little finger, picked in late spring to early summer, are stuffed through the small top, then covered in brine, dill and garlic and left in the season's sun to cure. They can be extracted only by cutting the bottle open, and are at their best when they are two or three days old, still alive with flavour and colour and just starting to turn. This is not how we make them at Honey & Co, for many reasons: first and foremost, we can't get the early-harvest little cucumbers; and we can't get the sun; also we are not sure what is the EU health and safety procedure when it comes to cola bottles, nor do we want to find out. But still, we pickle, and quite a lot; we use boring, sanitised jars and the best produce we can find. We prefer lighter pickles that retain as much of the original vegetable texture and flavour as possible, and we love having them before the main meal, as they get the juices going without ruining your appetite, and work a dream with booze.

Pickles

In most of these recipes we don't advise lengthy storage as these are fast pickles with a low salt or vinegar content – this helps the flavours stay fresh, but also means they will not keep long-term. 'Canned' in the current context simply means 'preserved'; we are not actually canning anything in the literal sense. But whatever you call them, these are good little numbers to keep in the fridge when you need a quick flavourful snack.

Cucumber pickle

I first tasted these pickles over ten years ago. A great lady of Turkish origins prepared them, then refused to give me the recipe. Later when I asked again, she pretended she didn't know what I was talking about, but I remembered. Years later I had something similar in a little diner in Galata, a beautiful neighbourhood in Istanbul, and recreated it at home. It is silly-simple but the flavour is everything you want from pickled cucumbers.

Serves 4–6 to nibble on

4 Lebanese cucumbers or 2 regular
  cucumbers (about 600g)
1 tsp salt
200ml cider vinegar
150ml water
4 tbsp caster sugar
3 tbsp white mustard seeds
2 bay leaves
3 sprigs of fresh dill
1 clove of garlic, peeled and sliced

We like to zebra our cucumbers. It isn't necessary, but it makes them look prettier and we think it produces a better texture. By zebra, we mean removing a few strips of the peel, lengthways, using a vegetable peeler so that the slices of cucumber have a pattern around the edge. Whether you choose to zebra them or not, slice the cucumbers about 2cm thick.

Place the slices of cucumber in a sieve that is resting over a bowl, and sprinkle with the salt. Mix together a little and then leave the cucumber to sit for at least 30 minutes and up to an hour, so that some of their juice is released.

In a small saucepan, heat the vinegar, water, sugar, mustard seeds and bay leaves, stirring gently until the sugar has completely dissolved. Do not let the liquid boil. The flavours of the bay and mustard seed will infuse the vinegar. Remove from the heat and allow to cool entirely.

Tip the infused vinegar (with the mustard seeds and bay leaves) into a bowl. Add the cucumber pieces (discarding the juice that has been released) along with the dill and garlic, then chill in the fridge. This is a fast pickle, so you can eat it after about 3 hours. It will keep for 8–10 days in the fridge, and will change dramatically during that time; the first few days will see it bright green and crunchy, and it will turn uglier in colour but better in flavour as days go by.

Sweet beetroot pickle

My mum is British; she was born and grew up in north London. The food I cook these days is far removed from the food she grew up with, nonetheless this is her recipe. I think it originally came from a Jewish cookbook she got when she went to Israel for the summer as a teenager and found herself in a camp in charge of cooking for another 30 hungry teenagers. The original called for boiling the beets in water until soft, but we prefer to roast ours, as in the following recipe.

Serves 4–6 to nibble on

2 tbsp salt
4–6 beetroots (about 300g)
90g light brown sugar
125ml red wine vinegar
  (we use a Greek Corinthian vinegar)
125ml water
½ tsp salt
3 cloves
1 stick of cinnamon
1 dried red chilli
2 bay leaves

Preheat the oven to 200°C/180°C fan/ gas mark 6.

Sprinkle the salt on the bottom of a roasting tin – it seems like a lot, but it is there to draw moisture, not to season. Place the whole beets, skin and all, on the salt and place in the centre of the oven for 30 minutes. Check whether they are cooked with a small knife – it should enter them easily. If there is any resistance, leave them in for an extra 10–15 minutes as necessary. The speed at which they cook depends on their freshness and so it is hard to be precise about cooking times. Remove the cooked beets from the salt and place them in a bowl. Allow them to cool.

With a little knife, top and tail the beet-roots, and then the skin should just rub off. It's best to use disposable gloves, if you have them, to stop your hands going pink. Cut the beetroots into wedges (each one can be cut into 8–10 wedges) and place in an airtight container.

Heat all the remaining ingredients together and bring to the boil. Pour over the beetroots, including all the spices, and seal the container. Leave at room temperature to cool, then place in the fridge.

The beetroots will be ready to eat the next day but will improve with time. If stored in an unopened airtight container, they can last for up to a month in the fridge, but once opened they should be eaten within 2 weeks.

Moroccan carrot pickle

A good friend introduced us to Daniel. A straight-talking New Yorker, publisher and poet, the bright white cloud of his hair is like a saint's halo, though I'm sure he is anything but. He liked these pickles very much and made us an offer so obscene we dare not repeat it here, and though we could not accept, we gave him the recipe for this pickle.

Serves 4–6 to nibble on

4–5 carrots, peeled (about 400g)
150ml white wine vinegar
100ml water
4 tbsp sugar
½ tsp salt
1½ tsp white mustard seeds
2 bay leaves
4 cloves
1 tbsp harissa paste

We like to score the carrots with five lines, lengthways, so that when they are sliced they look like little flowers. We use the hook on the end of our vegetable peeler, but you could buy a special channelling knife if you are into food gadgets. It's not essential to score them, though; they taste good either way. Slice the carrots thinly – about 2mm thick (you can use the blade of a food processor or a mandolin) – and put them in a bowl or airtight container.

In a small saucepan, combine the vinegar, water, sugar, salt, mustard seeds, bay leaves and cloves and bring to the boil. As soon as it has boiled, turn off the heat and add the harissa paste. Stir well and pour over the carrots while still hot. The liquid should cover the carrots entirely. If you are pouring into an airtight container, make sure to push your carrots down under the liquid before sealing. Leave to cool at room temperature and then place in the fridge.

The carrots will be ready to eat the next day but will improve with time. If stored in an unopened airtight container, they can last for up to a month in the fridge, but once opened they should be eaten within 2 weeks.

Canned peppers

I prefer the fleshy mouthful of regular bell peppers here; Sarit prefers the silky texture of the long ones, called Romano or Romero. If, like us, you have strong feelings about the qualities of different peppers, take a minute to congratulate yourself on having a very fortunate life.

For 4 as part of a mezze platter, but do double this recipe, treble it – have this in the fridge always

3–4 long red peppers
3 sprigs of fresh thyme
3 cloves of garlic, peeled and thinly sliced
a sprinkling of sea salt and freshly ground
    black pepper
2 tbsp red wine vinegar
2 tbsp good olive oil

Turn your oven on to grill at 250°C and set the peppers on a baking tray – you can line it with aluminium foil or a silicon baking sheet, but avoid parchment as it can catch fire. Wait till the grill is piping hot, then place the tray directly under it. It will take 4–5 minutes to burn the skin of the peppers (you want them to be going black), then carefully turn them and scorch the other side for another 4–5 minutes.

Quickly transfer the burnt offerings to a bowl and cover it with cling film, or do the same as my mum: throw them into a plastic bag and tie it – that way, once they have cooled, you can peel the peppers inside the bag, remove the flesh and leave the skins inside the bag to throw in the rubbish (clever lady).

Once the peppers are cool enough to handle, peel away the skin. It should just fall off. Don't be tempted to wash them or you will lose all the flavour. Tear each pepper into about six long strips. Set them in a bowl, add all the other ingredients and mix well.

The peppers will be ready within an hour but improve with time. They will keep just as they are in an airtight container in the fridge for a week. If you want to keep them for longer, place everything in a pot and bring to the boil, then seal in a sterilised jar.* They will keep for 2–3 weeks in the fridge like this, but should be consumed within a week once opened.

To sterilise the jar, preheat the oven to 200°C/180°C fan/gas mark 6. Wash the jar (and its lid) in hot soapy water and rinse well. Place on a baking tray and heat in the oven for 5 minutes. Alternatively pour boiling water into the clean jar, count to ten, then pour the water out and fill the jar immediately.

Canned artichokes

This is our version of the Turkish classic, artichokes cooked in olive oil. Not only are these great to eat by themselves, but they are also a base ingredient in artichokes and kashkaval with pine nuts (page 128). We wrote the recipe for large globe artichokes as they are more readily available, but the small violet ones work well in this recipe too, although you may need to reduce the cooking time.

2 lemons
240ml water
4–5 large globe artichokes
120ml white wine
1 large head of garlic, cut in half across
*   the bulb to expose all cloves*
4 sprigs of thyme
½ tsp whole peppercorns
½ tsp whole coriander seeds
½ tsp salt
240ml olive oil

First prepare the artichokes. Juice one and a half lemons and mix the juice with the water. Then remove the artichoke hearts. You do this by placing an artichoke on the chopping board, cutting the stem off as close to the base as you can, then holding it firmly at the thickest part and, with a sharp serrated knife, cutting straight down just above where you are holding (at the point where the artichoke starts to narrow again). This should expose the top of the heart and you should see the tiny pink leaves at the beginning of the choke. If they are not showing, cut another thin slice until you can see them, then turn the cut surface of the artichoke to face you. Use your knife and follow the pattern of the artichoke by cutting away all the green leaves so you are left with the white heart. Then, with a small paring knife, remove the last of the green leaves from the base and place the cleaned heart in the lemon water. Repeat with all the others.

Place the artichokes – chokes facing upwards – in a saucepan that fits them snugly, preferably in one layer. Fill the pan to half the height of the artichokes with the lemon water they have been soaking in and discard the rest. Slice the remaining half lemon and add to the pan along with everything else. Place on the stove on a medium-low heat and very slowly bring to the boil. Reduce the heat and continue cooking on a low heat for about 40 minutes until most of the liquid is gone and the artichokes are coated with the oil.

Pierce the centre of a choke to see if the tip of the knife goes in easily. If not, cook for a little longer. Leave to cool in the pan, then store with the cooking liquid in an airtight container. These will keep in the fridge for up to a week. Before serving, remove the choke – it will come out easily by pushing it with your finger or using a teaspoon.

The uses for these are many: you can serve them cut into wedges; you can skewer them with a cube of goats' cheese; you can slice them onto toasted bread; or you can use them in salads or in any other recipes in this book. We prefer to warm them slightly in the cooking liquid before serving.

Pink turnip pickle

Turnips are a strange phenomenon: no one ever seems to buy or eat them, yet almost every falafel joint, kebab shop and Middle Eastern restaurant serves these pink pickles. They are sulphurous and a bit funky at first taste, but completely addictive once you get over the initial shock. Serve them before or with rich, spicy meats, like lamb shawarma (page 209) or beef kofta (page 146), as they will cut through the fat nicely. They do benefit from being paired with mint, for flavour and beauty. To achieve that pretty pink, we use a little bit of beetroot – if you can, don't skip this stage. You can use the rest of the beetroot for one of the other recipes in the book.

**Serves 4–6
to nibble on**

*4 small turnips (about 400g)
2 thin slices of peeled beetroot
1 tsp salt
150ml white wine vinegar
150ml water
1 bay leaf
5 cloves*

Peel the turnips and dice them into 2cm cubes. Place in an airtight container with the beetroot slices and sprinkle with the salt. Allow to sit for 1 hour at room temperature.

Heat the vinegar, water, bay leaf and cloves until they come to the boil.

Remove from the heat immediately and pour over the turnips. Push the turnips down so they are all covered in liquid and seal the container. Leave to cool to room temperature, then place in the fridge.

The turnips will be ready to eat the next day but will improve with time. If stored in an unopened airtight container, they can last for up to a month in the fridge, but once opened they should be eaten within 2 weeks.

Turmeric cauliflower pickle

This isn't a fast pickle per se – it will take up to a week to mature fully and then needs to be transferred to the fridge to keep its crunch – but it is fast to make. You don't need to heat the pickling liquid as it would cook the cauliflower too quickly, and instead of crunchy flowers you would get wilted ones.

Serves 4–6 to nibble on

1 small head of cauliflower (about 300g), divided into small florets
1 tsp salt
1 tsp ground turmeric
2 tsp mustard seeds
2 tsp cumin seeds
1 whole dried red chilli
2 bay leaves
300ml water
100ml white wine vinegar

Place the cauliflower in a sterilised jar* and sprinkle with the salt and all the spices and herbs. Cover with the water and vinegar. Seal and place on a windowsill for 2–3 days, during which time the colour should deepen. Then place the jar in the fridge – the pickles are ready to eat once cold, but for full flavour wait another 2–3 days. They can last for up to a month in the fridge, but once opened they should be eaten within 2 weeks.

* *To sterilise the jar, preheat the oven to 200°C/180°C fan/gas mark 6. Wash the jar (and its lid) in hot soapy water and rinse well. Place on a baking tray and heat in the oven for 5 minutes. Alternatively pour boiling water into the clean jar, count to ten, then pour the water out and fill the jar immediately.*

Pickled chillies

This is another kebab shop staple. We used to buy these in and when our supplier ran out we thought nothing of it, till we faced an uproar and disappointment from our regulars, especially Adam, a young writer who comes in for breakfast meetings. After a few horrible attempts, we came up with this good recipe. If you are an addict, knock yourself out.

16 long green chillies
1 litre water
1 tsp salt
1 tsp sugar
white wine vinegar
salt water (1 tsp salt dissolved
  in 250ml water)

Pierce each chilli 3–4 times with a toothpick. Bring the water, salt and sugar to the boil, add the chillies and boil until they soften.

Remove chillies from the cooking liquid and pack tightly into a sterilised jar.* Cover halfway with vinegar, then top up with the salt water (depending on the size of the jar and chillies, you may not use all the salt water, or you may need a bit more). Make sure the chillies are submerged entirely, then seal the jar and place on a windowsill in direct sun to ferment for a week, after which they will be ready to eat.

You can keep the sealed jar in a cool, dark place for up to a month, but once opened you should keep the jar in the fridge and consume the chillies within a week.

* To sterilise the jar, preheat the oven to 200°C/180°C fan/gas mark 6. Wash the jar (and its lid) in hot soapy water and rinse well. Place on a baking tray and heat in the oven for 5 minutes. Alternatively pour boiling water into the clean jar, count to ten, then pour the water out and fill the jar immediately.

Bread.

I wanted to serve only one type of bread at our restaurant and I had visions of the flat, round, golden loaves that were stacked at the Bukhari bakery at the entrance to the market in Jerusalem – decorated with criss-cross cuts and nigella seeds, always oven-fresh, easy to tear and dunk into dips, soups or sauces. Like sponge, it soaks up any tasty liquid on the plate, leaving it squeaky clean and making for a very happy mouthful. We have played with various recipes, looking mostly online for Bukhari ones. We did stumble across a good website dedicated to the food of Uzbekistan that mentions the bread of the Bukhari Jews, but when the recipe called for a custom-built clay oven and a fair bit of goat fat, we decided to improvise. We ended up with quite a good recipe, and I was pleased with the thought that this would be our signature bread.

Our first day of trade was coming close. We stayed up the night before, prepping everything – me in the kitchen, Sarit at the pastry and upstairs our devoted coffee guy, Robert Henry (or Henry Robert, we still don't know which is his first and which his last), refusing to give up on reconditioning our coffee machine. The day itself was a bit of a blur. Our idea of creating a little service kitchen upstairs went up in smoke – quite literally – when the portable electric hob I was cooking eggs on exploded, leaving our first customers teary-eyed and gasping for air. We had to move the breakfast pass to Sarit downstairs, while I stayed with our waitress Rachael upstairs, on my first day ever as a waiter.

Clumsy, disorganised and always saying the wrong thing, waiting tables was not a natural thing for me. Luckily the magical Rachael was completely unfazed, pouring drinks and sorting bills, taking it all in her stride and still finding time to charm whoever walked in, as she still does. I, on the other hand, was bumping into things, knocking drinks onto people and floor, and running up and down inefficiently (a move that is now my trademark). Downstairs Sarit was handling the kitchen with typical calm and control, gliding elegantly between the kitchen and the pastry.

When the smoke subsided and the situation calmed down a bit, Rachael realised things would be easier without me and sent me downstairs to the kitchen, where I took a proud glimpse at our first loaf of bread. I noticed Sarit had a row of little dough balls on her pastry bench, proving.

I asked, 'What are these?'

'Yeah… I'm making pitta. Why aren't you upstairs helping Rachael? All I see you do is run up and down inefficiently.'

'Pitta? I thought we were only making one type of bread. You know we really don't have time to make pitta.'

'Yeah, well, you can't have a Middle Eastern restaurant without pitta,' she said in a tone that ended the conversation.

And of course she is right. You can't have a Middle Eastern restaurant without pitta.

We now make three or four types of bread on a daily basis. We are proud of them all, but it's pitta that everyone asks for.

Some general notes on our bread recipes

- We always use strong white flour.

- We use fine table salt.

- All your ingredients should be at room temperature.

- The water can be lukewarm.

- I prefer to use fresh yeast. My friend and colleague Bridgette says it's easy to obtain in the real world by walking up to the bakery counter in any large supermarket or bakery and asking to buy some. However I have given dried yeast measurements and methods as well, just in case.

- I always preheat the oven to a high setting when I am preparing the dough. It brings the kitchen temperature up closer to Middle Eastern levels and helps the dough to rise nicely. Considering the price of electricity, though, you may just want to prove the dough in a nice warm place until it's ready to bake.

- It's hard to give exact timings for proving dough as there are so many variables, from the temperature of the ingredients and the room, to the moisture in the air to the freshness of the yeast. As a general rule, however, the dough in each of the following recipes should take between one and a half to three hours at each proving stage.

- There are a few ways to judge if your dough is proved:

  - It will have more or less doubled in size.

  - It should be soft but firm and bounce back when you touch it.

  - It should retain its shape, but just be bigger and more taut.

- Make sure the oven is heated to the correct temperature before you put your bread in to bake.

- Once baked, bread is best cooled on a rack, to allow steam to escape from underneath.

Pitta

It is really the easiest thing in the world to make pitta bread. You just need to have faith in heat and air. You can make the dough a day in advance if you have time – it helps the flavour develop and makes the pitta fluffier – but it works well doing it all the same day too. Make more than you need and freeze them, as they keep well if frozen. That way you can just quickly pop one in the toaster and have it with hummus, or use it in a bread salad.

Makes 10 pitta breads

500g strong white flour, plus extra for dusting
1 tsp sugar (plus a pinch if using dried yeast)
1½ tsp salt
20g fresh yeast or 2 tsp dried yeast (fresh is better)
300–400ml warm water (just warmer than your fingertips)
2 tbsp olive oil

If you have a mixer with a dough attachment, use it. If not, you can use a large bowl. Mix together the flour, sugar and salt. If you are lucky and have fresh yeast, crumble it straight into your flour and mix to combine. If you are using dried yeast, place it in a cup and add 100ml of the warm water and the extra pinch of sugar. Mix with the tip of your finger and leave it to sit until a foam forms on the top, then pour it over the flour.

Start adding the warm water to the flour, a little at a time, mixing in circular motions until the dough starts to clump together. Give it a good mix and see if it will form a ball. If there is still some flour residue in the bottom of the bowl, add a little more water, but only a small amount, as you want it to just come together. Don't worry if there are some lumps at this stage.

If kneading by hand, this is the time to get some energy. Use a clean, flat surface and try not to add any flour. Throw the dough

around a bit and then smooth it out, working it again and again. If you are using a machine, this stage will be easy: just let it turn on a medium speed until the dough looks smooth and tight.

Add the oil and knead to combine. At first everything will become very slippery and it will seem as if it will never come together. But have faith; it will. And the final texture will be silky smooth.

Cover the bowl with cling film. If you are baking the pitta breads the next day, keep the dough in the fridge for the night. Make sure to put it in a container at least three times larger than the dough, as it will grow. If you want to bake them today, allow the dough to rest for a minimum of 1 hour at room temperature.

Place your heaviest baking tray in the middle of your oven (if you have a baking stone, even better) and preheat the oven to its highest setting – if you have a fan-assisted setting, use it.

Cut the dough into ten evenly-sized balls of approximately 80g each – they will be about the size of a clementine at this stage, but will grow to the size of a small orange before you flatten them. Roll each one between your palm and the table without using any flour; you want to press down on the dough and make circles with your palm. The dough will start to resist the pressure and will form a tight ball. Place each ball on a lightly floured tray, leaving a little space between each one. Allow to rest, uncovered, for 10–15 minutes. This will allow the gluten to rest before rolling out, and the dough will start to prove. If the room is very cold you may need to wait half an hour, but usually if you have turned the oven up to its highest setting, the room will be quite hot already.

Dust your workbench with flour and, using a rolling pin, roll out each pitta until it is very thin – about 0.5cm. I usually roll one way and then turn the dough over and roll the other way to get a nice even shape. You can use a fair amount of flour when rolling, as you don't want the dough to stick. The size you're aiming for is that of a starter plate. If your bench isn't large, you can place the rolled ones back on the proving tray until you bake them.

Once the pitta breads are all rolled out, the fun begins. Very carefully place them – as many dough rounds as will fit – flat on the hot tray in the oven. The best way is to use a bread paddle or a wide metal spatula: there is a knack to flicking the paddle back so that each pitta slides off without losing its shape. You may need to practise, but hey, that is true for everything in life. Don't take the tray out of the oven, as it will lose heat. Quickly shut the oven door.

Look through the oven's glass door, if it has one: the pitta breads will puff up like pillows. This will take 2–3 minutes, depending on how hot your oven gets. Once they have puffed up, quickly remove them. They are not supposed to colour much and don't need turning.

You can allow them to cool slightly on a wire rack before stacking, but don't wait until they are cold, as they start to dry out quickly. Stack them in one or two piles and cover with cling film or put them in a sealed bag. This will help them steam a little and stay really moist.

If you are not going to consume them within the next 12 hours, I suggest placing them in the freezer once cooled.

Bukhari bread

A city on the Silk Road, Bukhara gave its name to all Jewish communities in central Asia, from the Caspian Sea to modern-day Pakistan. The food of these people is an undiscovered treasure, delicious and abundant with stone fruit, nuts, herbs and sweet-scented spice. This is one such food to fill your home with the good smell of nigella seeds and bread baking, and your heart with pride at its outer and inner beauty.

Makes 1 large loaf

30g fresh yeast or 3 tsp dried yeast
  (fresh is better)
150ml warm water
2 tbsp sugar
500g strong white flour
1 egg
2 tsp salt
3 tbsp sunflower oil, plus 1 tbsp for oiling
  the dough (and a little extra)
1 tbsp nigella seeds or sesame seeds,
  to garnish

Mix the yeast with the water and sugar and set aside until it starts to froth.

In a large bowl mix the flour, egg, salt and sunflower oil. When the yeast mix has frothed, pour it into the flour mixture and work it all together to a smooth dough. You may need to add a little more water as you go, until the dough comes together into a ball.

Oil the dough ball all over with the additional tablespoon of oil, then cover the bowl with cling film and leave in a warm place to double in size. Preheat your oven to 240°C/220°C fan/gas mark 9.

Knock the dough back so all the air is pushed out and the texture is smooth and subtle. You shouldn't need to add any extra flour for this stage, and you can do it in the same bowl it was proving in. Place the dough on a lightly-floured baking tray, then shape into a large, flat oblong of roughly the same height as the first joint of your thumb (i.e. about 3–4cm thick).

Cover very loosely with cling film or a damp cloth. Again allow it to double in size – it should be at least the height of your full thumb when proved.

With a pair of sharp scissors, go all Edward Scissorhands on it – holding the scissors perpendicular to the dough, start snipping it every inch or so into little peaks. Brush with a little more oil and sprinkle the seeds on top.

Place in the centre of the oven for 10 minutes, then open the door carefully, turn the tray and reduce the heat to 200°C/180°C fan/gas mark 6. Bake for an extra 6–8 minutes until nicely browned. Remove from the oven to a cooling rack. Eat it or freeze it on the day of baking as it will not keep well for the next day.

Potato bread

The unique flavour and texture of this bread comes from letting the yeast gorge itself on a mush of potato and sugar, a diet which makes it particularly happy and jumpy, as it would anyone. The super-spongy texture is terrific for dipping and dunking, but it is also a great bread for sandwiches and delicious toasted, with a little olive oil.

Makes a 20–22cm round

1 large potato (about 125g)
300ml water
20g fresh yeast or 1½ tsp dried yeast
    (fresh is better)
1 tsp sugar
250g strong white flour, plus 100g for
    the second kneading
2 tsp salt
2 tbsp olive oil, plus extra for oiling the tin
    and dough

Peel the potato and cut into large dice; how big isn't important, just make sure all the pieces are similar in size so they cook in the same time. Cover with the water and boil until the potatoes are very soft. Allow to cool in the liquid – you want to proceed when the liquid is just warm. If you prefer to boil the potatoes in advance, then I suggest you heat the liquid slightly before continuing. Strain the potatoes, but measure out 150g of the cooking liquid, as you will need it for the bread.

Pour the reserved liquid back in with the potato, add the yeast and the sugar and blitz together – you can use a potato ricer if you don't own a stick blender or a food processor. It should create a gloopy, sticky paste. Sprinkle the first amount of flour (250g) all over the paste and then sprinkle the salt on top of that.

Set it aside in a warm place until the mix begins to bubble up and cracks appear in the flour. Mix it all together. This is a very sticky mix and I hate touching it with my hands, so either use a machine or a large spoon. Work the dough in circular motions until it is all combined. It will seem very wet, but this is totally normal. Cover the surface with the remaining 100g of flour, and allow to rest in a warm place until doubled in size.

Start mixing the dough and add the olive oil. Again, it is best to use a big spoon or an electric mixer to bring the dough together. It will resemble a strange glue that doesn't go shiny or supple; it just flops there, looking like a huge mistake... Don't worry, it's the result you are looking for. Oil a 20–22cm round tin (at least 4–5cm deep) or use an ovenproof frying pan. Scrape all the dough into the tin and, with some extra olive oil on your hands, smooth the dough down.

Now it is time to turn your oven on to preheat: set it at 250°C/230°C fan/gas mark 9.

Allow the bread to prove in a warm place until it has doubled in size. You can sprinkle it with sea salt just before baking, if you want. Place on the upper-middle shelf of the oven and set a timer for 10 minutes. Once the timer goes, carefully open the oven, turn the tray and close the door again. Reduce the oven heat to 220°C/200°C fan/gas mark 7 and set the timer for another 10 minutes. Again open the oven and turn the tray, checking that the bread is not colouring too quickly – it should have a lovely golden crust at this stage. Reduce the heat again, this time to 190°C/170°C fan/gas mark 5, and bake for the last 10 minutes.

Remove from the oven carefully and flip onto a rack to cool. This bread will keep well until the next day, but I doubt it will get the chance.

Ashtanur – griddle bread

This is the most basic and probably most ancient form of bread. It has many names, *ashtanur* being the Jerusalem moniker and the one which sounds best to us, but in my grandmother Esther's house it was called *saloof*. Her kitchen was divided in two – at the front was a shiny new kitchen with all mod cons and state of the art equipment. Food was not allowed there, cooking was forbidden – that one was for show. At the back she had a tiny little scullery she had turned into a galley kitchen, where all the real cooking was done. Before any family gathering she would barricade herself in there for days, boiling and roasting and making stacks of *saloof* for the freezer. She cooked it in the middle of the night, as the days were too hot to be cooped up there with a red-hot skillet. You can make the dough in advance if you wish and keep it refrigerated to cold-prove until you are ready to bake. Any bread that is left over can be wrapped in cling film or a plastic ziplock bag for future heating and eating, or left to dry and become tasty crackers – an added bonus.

Makes 6–7 flat breads

250g strong flour
½ tsp salt
7g fresh yeast or ½ tsp dried yeast
½ tsp honey (or sugar)
60ml + about 60ml warm water
1 tbsp vegetable oil, plus extra for oiling
   and rolling

Mix the flour and salt in a big bowl. Dissolve the yeast and honey (or sugar) in the first 60ml of warm water and set aside until it starts to foam.

Pour the foaming water-yeast mixture and the oil into the flour and mix, bringing it all together. Add as much of the additional water as you need to get a good even dough, then start kneading until it becomes supple and shiny. Drizzle with some extra oil on the top, cover the bowl with cling film and set aside until the dough doubles in volume, or place in the fridge for the next day.

Oil your workbench and turn the dough out. Divide into six or seven balls of approximately 50g each and roll them in the oil, making sure each one has a nice coating of it. Leave them on the counter for 10 minutes to rest. Now is the time to set the griddle pan on the stove to heat up.

Start stretching the dough balls. The best way is to oil your hands, then press the dough down to flatten and spread it with your hands until it is as thin as you can get it – you should almost see the work surface through it.

Lift the first stretched dough ball carefully and pop it on the hot griddle pan. It will take about a minute or two to colour, then flip it, cook for 10 seconds and remove from the pan. Put the next one on and repeat the process. Stack them while they are hot and wrap them in cling film to serve later the same day, freeze once cooled or eat immediately.

Lavoush

This bread is a staple in Eastern Turkey, Georgia and Armenia. It is now a London staple as well, as every restaurant we have worked in has seemed to serve a version of it, and it's easy to see why – it's crispy, light and works with everything. At the restaurant we sometimes serve it with soft things that need scooping, like taramasalata or baba ganoush (page 85). The topping should be complementary in flavour and there is no end to the variations – za'atar is good; all kinds of seeds in all kinds of combinations; crushed nuts; chilli flakes; most spices; crunchy sea salt and so on. We like to bake a whole sheet and break it into freeform uneven shards, but if you need something less rustic-looking, cut it before baking into whatever shape you want.

180g strong white flour
14g soft butter
a pinch of sugar
½ tsp salt
60–80ml water
1 egg for brushing
your choice of topping for sprinkling

Will make 4 large pieces – good for 4–6 people to eat with dips

Mix the flour, butter, sugar and salt together and start adding the water until you have a really heavy, dry dough that just comes together, but isn't soft or subtle. Bring it to a rough ball and wrap it in cling film. Place it in the fridge to rest for a minimum of 1 hour – you can leave it for up to 2 days.

Heat your oven to 190°C/170°C fan/gas mark 5. Remove the cling film and divide the dough into four. On a clean surface, roll each quarter as thinly as you can get it. You can use a pasta machine if you own one, but rolling by hand works just as well. Keep turning it over and rotating the dough, so that you give it a good working as you are rolling. If you made the dough dry enough, you will not need any extra flour for rolling, but if it does start to stick, dust the surface with a little flour.

Lift each piece of thinly-rolled dough carefully and lay on a baking sheet. If you only have deep trays, flip them over and use them upside down, as the bread needs to be baked on a surface without sides for better air circulation. Brush the top with some beaten egg and sprinkle with the topping of your choice. Bake for 10–12 minutes, until the bread turns golden. Remove to a cooling rack to crisp up and once they are cold place in a sealed container. These will keep for a couple of days, but are so moreish that there isn't much chance of that happening.

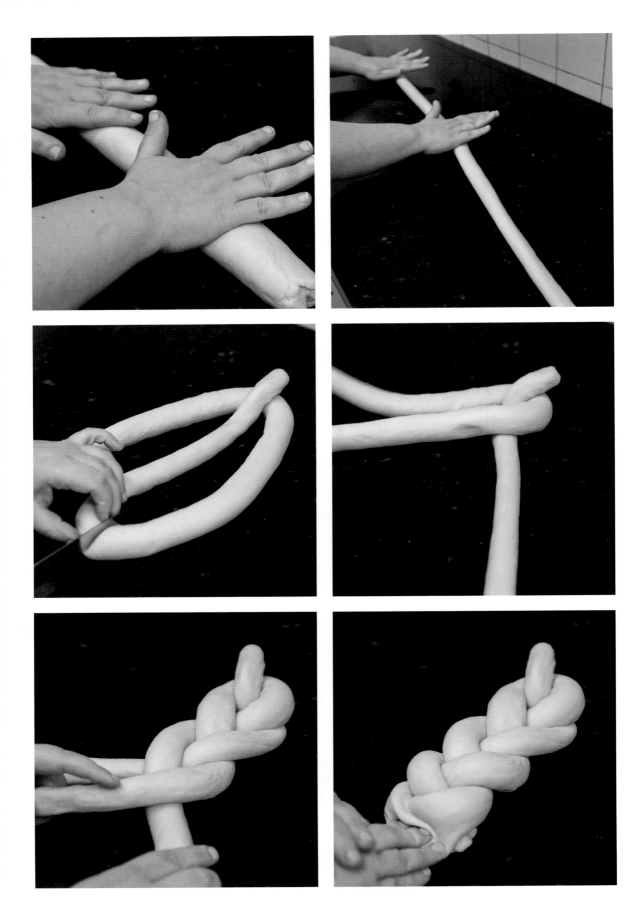

Milk bun

This bread is the love child of the Jewish *cholla* and the French *brioche*: it is lighter and smoother than the former without being as rich as the latter. And like both its parents, it provides a feeling of both comfort and luxury, everyday and special occasion at the same time. The plait shape not only looks beautiful but makes it easy to tear a piece with your hand rather than slice, which is just how it should be eaten.

Will make one loaf, which is enough for 4–6 people

50ml + about 60ml warm milk
20g fresh yeast or 1 tbsp dried yeast
25g sugar
250g strong flour
½ tsp salt
1 whole egg
50g soft butter
milk or beaten egg to glaze
poppy seeds and salt to sprinkle (optional)

Heat 50ml of the milk until it's warm to the touch, then add the yeast and sugar and set aside until it starts to foam.

In a large bowl, combine the flour, salt, egg and butter. Pour in the foaming milk-yeast mixture and mix to a smooth dough, adding as much of the additional milk as is needed. It should come together to a really smooth dough, and you need to work it until it goes all shiny. You can do this easily by hand, but if you prefer you can use a mixer bowl with a dough hook. Once the dough is all shiny, cover the bowl with cling film and leave in a warm place to prove until doubled in size.

Remove the dough from the bowl and place on a clean, flat surface – I don't usually add any more flour, but if it sticks, use a little. Start rolling the dough to a long snake. It is best to roll from the middle outwards, repeating until the dough is approximately 75cm long.

Cut 25cm off one end of the dough snake and set aside. Arrange the remaining length as an upside down letter 'U' on a lined baking tray. Lay the 25cm length in a straight line down the middle of the 'U', with one end resting on top of the dough at the centre of the curve (this will form a little top-knot at one end of the finished plait). Now plait the three strips of dough as you would hair or string, but don't tuck it tight: leave it loose so that the dough has room to prove. Cover loosely with cling film and leave in a warm place until it doubles in size.

Preheat your oven to 220°C/200°C fan/ gas mark 7.

Carefully remove the cling film and brush the dough all over with milk or beaten egg and, if you wish, sprinkle with some poppy seeds and salt. Make sure your oven is hot and place the plait on the middle shelf for 8 minutes. Reduce the heat to 200°C/180°C fan/gas mark 6, open the door carefully and turn the tray. Bake for a further 8 minutes, then reduce the heat again to 180°C/160°C fan/gas mark 4 for the last 8 minutes.

Remove from the oven and allow to cool a little before eating. This bread is best eaten as soon after baking as possible, but makes great toast the next day.

Dips, Spreads & Purées.

Where we come from hummus is so revered it is prepared in shops that sell only that, by people who have mastered the art over decades, if not generations. The loyalty and emotions these places evoke are very similar to those you may have for your football team or your religion. And Sarit and I have very different opinions on the subject: my Jerusalem palate demands the pure and austere version which tastes strongly of chickpeas and little else, while my wife craves something different altogether, rich and creamy with tahini, and with plenty of cumin and lemon to cut through it. With all the tension that comes with restaurant life, this is one issue we thought we could do without, and so we decided to avoid the subject altogether and not serve hummus at all. I still think it was the right thing to do – it shows humility before the old traditions, as well as our ambition to bring a different view of Middle Eastern food to the London table.

The act of using bread to dip and scoop things up seemed so typical of every cuisine in the region, and of the way people eat that kind of food, that we knew dips had to be part of the mezze we offered. We've prepared dips out of pretty much everything – some traditional and others not so much, all delicious

(we thought) – but that was not what the people wanted. The people wanted hummus, ignoring the fact it was not on the menu and naturally assuming that a Middle Eastern place worth its salt would give them a bit of hummus and bread with their meal. Our first concession was a dish of heavily spiced lamb mince with pine nuts and herbs, sitting atop a plateful of hummus. This 'meat hummus' dish created such a frenzy among our customers that we struggled to sell anything else, and vegetarians would ask for 'the meat hummus without the meat'. Those who did order a different main would ask for 'just a bit of hummus to start' or 'on the side' – the floodgates had opened. I am not sure if the combination of chickpeas, tahini, lemon and salt creates a chemical reaction in the brain that makes the substance so crave-able, but it is definitely more than the sum of its parts.

We have now reached a strange equilibrium – hummus is not on the menu, but there is a big pot of chickpeas on the stove every morning, and there is a fresh batch of hummus prepared and sold every day. The version we agreed on is very well balanced and contains just a few ingredients: chickpeas, tahini, lemon, garlic, salt and – after many fights with Sarit and Julia – a little bit of cumin.

Hummus

Enough for 4–6 to have as a starter portion, or you could make half this amount to share as a mezze

250g dried chickpeas, soaked overnight in plenty of water so they double in volume
1 tsp bicarbonate of soda
3 cloves of garlic, peeled
250g tahini paste
½ tsp ground cumin
1 tsp salt, plus more to taste
1 tbsp lemon juice, plus more to taste

Drain the soaked chickpeas and check for any small stones or damaged chickpeas, discarding any you find. Tip the chickpeas into your largest pan and cover with plenty of fresh cold water. Bring to the boil and skim off the foam that forms. Allow to boil for 5 minutes, then skim again. Add the bicarbonate of soda and mix well; the whole thing will bubble up like a volcano. Skim it thoroughly, then cook at a steady simmer, skimming regularly – this will give you a much clearer, paler result. It will take about 30–40 minutes for the chickpeas to soften entirely. The best indication will be the foam, which will become really thick and yellow. This is the time to check the chickpeas; scoop a couple out and try them: they should melt in your mouth without any resistance.

Remove the pan from the heat and drain the chickpeas into a colander sitting on a bowl or jug, as you want to retain the cooking liquid. Tip the chickpeas into a separate bowl – the drained weight should be about 600g. To this you want to return 250ml of the cooking liquid. It is important to do this while everything is still hot, as you get a much smoother texture – if you leave the chickpeas and liquid to cool before blending, the texture is chunkier.

Add the garlic cloves and blitz with a stick blender or food processor until the mixture is really smooth. It will look more like chickpea soup than a dip, but don't worry! Add the rest of the ingredients and continue blitzing until everything is well combined. Cover the surface of the hummus directly with cling film to avoid a skin developing while it is cooling. It will still look too runny at this stage, but will thicken as it cools, and you may even need to add a touch of water to loosen it when it is cold. The final texture should be lovely and creamy, easy to scoop up in a piece of pitta bread. If you end up with a solid mass, just mix in a couple of tablespoons of water to loosen.

You can place it in the fridge until serving or just leave it to cool at room temperature. We prefer making and eating hummus on the same day, but it will keep in an airtight container in the fridge for up to 2 days (avoid keeping it any longer, as chickpeas can easily start to ferment).

When you are ready to serve, taste and adjust the salt and lemon levels to your own preference. Spread the hummus on a plate and top with ground cumin or smoky paprika or chopped parsley or chopped coriander or roasted pine nuts or olive oil or za'atar or sumac, or all of the above, or none of them. Serve with fresh pitta, crackers, onion wedges, hard-boiled eggs, vegetable sticks or just teaspoons…

Mashawsha

This is a variation on hummus, and even though it uses almost all of the same ingredients, it somehow tastes completely different. It is a great starter, and in Israel it is the ultimate late Saturday breakfast after a night out. It is looser than hummus and the dressing is really important, so don't skip it. We love serving it with slow-cooked eggs, a preparation that our kitchen crew calls dinosaur eggs (page 76) for reasons of their own.

Enough for 4–6 as a starter, or you could make half this quantity to share as a mezze

250g dried chickpeas, soaked overnight in plenty of water so they double in volume
1 tsp bicarbonate of soda
1 tsp table salt
1 tsp ground cumin
2 tbsp lemon juice
2 tbsp tahini paste

For the dressing
1 tbsp lemon juice
3 cloves of garlic, peeled and finely chopped
1 green chilli, finely chopped (I use the seeds too, for spiciness)
1 small bunch of parsley, chopped (about 15–20g)

Drain the soaked chickpeas and check for any small stones or damaged chickpeas, discarding any you find. Tip the chickpeas into your largest pan and cover with plenty of fresh cold water. Bring to the boil and skim off the foam that forms. Allow to boil for 5 minutes, then skim again. Add the bicarbonate of soda and mix well; the whole thing will bubble up like a volcano. Skim it thoroughly, then cook at a steady simmer, skimming regularly – this will give you a much clearer, paler result. It will take about 30–40 minutes for the chickpeas to soften entirely. The best indication will be the foam, which will become really thick and yellow. This is the time to check the chickpeas; scoop a couple out and try them: they should melt in your mouth without any resistance.

Remove the pan from the heat and drain the chickpeas into a colander sitting on a bowl or jug, as you want to retain the cooking liquid. Tip the chickpeas into a separate bowl – the drained weight should be about 600g. To this you want to return 160ml of the cooking liquid while everything is still hot.

Mix in the salt, cumin and lemon juice. Mash the mixture using a stick blender or a potato masher – if you're using a stick blender, plunge it in for a second in a couple of places then stop, so that most of the texture stays chunky. Now use a spoon to fold in the tahini paste and allow to cool a little – but this is traditionally served warm, so don't place it in the fridge.

Mix the dressing ingredients together and drizzle all over the *mashawsha*. You could top with wedges of dinosaur eggs (page 76) and, if you want, a touch of paprika for colour.

Dinosaur eggs

The recipe for these eggs originates from the Jewish ban on cooking on the Sabbath, which gave birth to many dishes throughout the Jewish world, dishes that would cook slowly from Friday afternoon till Saturday lunch. Traditionally the eggs would be placed in a pot with a big joint of meat and some pulses and grains, then left to cook overnight. The eggs would be pulled out and eaten for breakfast, and the rest of the dish kept warm for lunch. The slow cooking of the eggs makes the whites go a light brown colour and gives the eggs a soft, yielding texture. We use the cheats' way to make them here – without the joint of meat – but the texture is still something completely different to any egg you will have tried, and they are very pretty.

4–6 eggs
enough water to cover
1 tsp salt
1 tbsp coffee grounds
1 tea bag

Allow 1–2 per person (up to you – we prefer more than 1 per person)

Place the eggs with the water and salt in an ovenproof pan on the stove and bring to the boil, then simmer for 3 minutes. Remove the eggs from the pan and crack the shells all over with the back of a spoon – but try to leave them intact. Return the eggs to the water, add the coffee grounds and tea bag and place in the oven for 2 hours at between 180°C/160°C fan/gas mark 4 and 200°C/180°C fan/gas mark 6

(we usually make these when we are using the oven for some other slow-cooked dish, so we cook them at the temperature that dish calls for). Check the eggs every 30 minutes to see whether they are still submerged, and top up the water if need be.

Cool and peel them before serving. These go really well with *mashawsha* (page 75), but you can also use them to fill a sandwich or to add something extra to your daily salad.

Matbucha

Matbucha simply means 'cooked' in Arabic and this is what it is – a savoury, smoky, sweet cooked vegetable jam with endless uses: as a dip at the start of a meal with bread and oil; in a sandwich with any kind of cheese; as a sauce in which to cook fish or seafood, or eggs for Middle Eastern breakfast-favourite *shakshuka*; or as a relish with anything grilled. It is a great staple, so it's worth doubling up the recipe. The only reason we stopped making this in the restaurant was out of deference to our beloved kitchen porter Pierre Paolo, a scrawny boy from Sardinia who captured our hearts with his endless energy and crooked smile. He would slave away trying to restore our pots to usable form after each batch we made – *matbucha* will always burn, which is what gives it the smoky flavour. We think it is still worth making as it really is delicious and versatile. Just do as Pierre Paolo does and put some cold water in the burnt pan, add a teaspoon of bicarbonate of soda or baking powder and place on the stove to simmer for 5–10 minutes, after which you should be able to return the pan to its former condition.

For 4–6 to share as a mezze

1 tbsp olive oil
1 onion, peeled and diced (about 100g)
1 green pepper, seeded and diced
   (about 120g)
1 red pepper, seeded and diced (about 120g)
4 cloves of garlic, peeled and thinly sliced
1 green or red chilli, thinly sliced (keep the
   seeds if you want a kick, or discard if you
   prefer a milder flavour)
¼ tsp + ¼ tsp salt, plus more to taste
½ tsp whole caraway seeds
½ tsp whole cumin seeds
3–4 plum tomatoes, coarsely chopped
   (about 350g)
2 slices of lemon
a pinch of chilli flakes, to finish (if you wish)

Place a heavy-bottomed pan on a high heat. Add the olive oil and onion, and stir around while the onion cooks for a minute. Then add the peppers, garlic, chilli and first quarter-teaspoon of salt. Mix well and continue cooking for 4–5 minutes, keeping the heat high, until everything starts to soften.

Tip in the caraway and cumin seeds and stir to combine. The pan will start to blacken – this is fine, as it is what will give the dip its smokiness. Add the tomatoes and the second quarter-teaspoon of salt, combine thoroughly and allow to cook for 2 minutes on high. Stir in the lemon slices, then lower the heat and simmer until you have a thick rich paste, making sure to scrape the bottom of the pan once in a while. This should take about 30 minutes, and I like to set a timer every 5 minutes to remind me to stir.

Taste to see if you need to add a little more salt and – if it is missing some heat – add the chilli. You can use it straight away as a sauce, or allow it to cool before serving as a dip, relish or sandwich filling. *Matbucha* will keep for up to a week in an airtight container in the fridge, and freezes and defrosts without harm.

Butternut & tahini dip with roasted hazelnuts

This recipe brings together two great ladies who have never met. We picked up the original recipe from a cookbook by Sherry Ansky (a most gifted cook and even more gifted writer), and though we prepared it many times with great success, we got the best results with the heather honey we received from our good friend who is now our publisher, Elizabeth. This is a simple preparation with few ingredients, but it is one of the best recipes in this book. The hazelnuts are there for their good looks and crunch, and they add a special nuttiness to the whole thing, but of course you can omit them if you wish.

Serves 6–8 to share as a mezze

1 large butternut squash (about 700–800g, to give 600g once peeled and deseeded)
½ tsp salt
60g tahini paste
2 tsp heather honey
30g whole hazelnuts, salted, roasted and roughly chopped

Peel the butternut squash and scoop out the seeds. Because I have small hands, peeling a whole squash can be quite hard, and I find it easier to cut it into wedges and peel each wedge separately. Cut the peeled butternut into large dice (about 2cm square). Try to make the pieces evenly-sized so that they cook in the same time. Put in a heavy-bottomed saucepan with a lid, sprinkle with the salt and cover.

Place the saucepan on the stove on a very low heat and set a timer for 10 minutes. Don't be tempted to remove the lid before then, as you want some steam to start developing. When the timer sounds, lift the lid and give the squash a good stir, then cover again and set the timer for a further 10 minutes. I repeat this four or five times. You will see the progress – the cubes will start to break down and become a purée. If some of the butternut sticks to the bottom of the pan, scrape it with the tip of a wooden spoon, as there is so much flavour down there. You want to stop cooking once the squash has formed a thick paste with no visible water content.

Remove the pan from the stove and add the tahini and honey. Mix well and allow to cool before adjusting the flavour with more honey or salt, as it will change when cool. You may need to add a little water to get a lighter consistency – it's a matter of personal preference how light or thick you want to make it.

Sprinkle the hazelnuts over the dip just before serving. Any leftover dip will keep in an airtight container in the fridge for up to 2 days.

Celeriac purée with burnt yogurt

This is a slightly Middle Eastern treatment for what we consider a very British vegetable. The celeriac we get in Israel is a tight, angry, sandy little root – nothing like the large, generous, creamy-fleshed beauties we discovered when we came to this country. To us this is a truly exotic vegetable.

For 4–6 to share as a mezze

1 small celeriac head (about 500g)
2 tbsp olive oil
6 cloves of garlic, peeled
2 sprigs of thyme
1 tsp sea salt
10g butter
100g natural yogurt

Peel the celeriac and cut into small dice. Place in a heavy-bottomed pan with the oil, whole garlic cloves, thyme sprigs and salt. Start on a high heat for about 5–6 minutes to give the dice some colour, then reduce the heat and cook until they go really soft (about 10 minutes). If they catch too much on the bottom of the pan, add 1–2 tablespoons of water and continue cooking until soft.

Tip the cooked celeriac and garlic into a bowl and remove the thyme sprigs. Put the butter in the empty pan and return it to the stove on a high heat to melt it, then continue heating until it starts to go golden-brown. This develops a very different flavour, so don't be scared to let it happen.

Remove from the heat and pour onto the celeriac dice. Add the yogurt and use a stick blender (or food processor) to purée everything together to a chunky dip. Don't make it too smooth, as getting a little surprise cube of soft celeriac is the best bit.

This is best eaten at room temperature. If you want to store it, just pop it in an airtight container in the fridge (where it will keep well for 2–3 days) and allow it to come up to room temperature before serving.

Dips, Spreads & Purées.

Courgette dip with yogurt & mint

This preparation – simple though it is – is one of the nicest things you can do with courgettes, a vegetable with more texture than flavour. We picked up this little number in Istanbul, where they mix the cooked pulp with a traditional burnt butter and yogurt sauce. We don't normally mess with tradition, but in this case we think that this dip is good enough with plain yogurt.

**Serves 4–6
to share as
a mezze**

600g courgettes (about 4–5)
6 cloves of garlic (about 30g)
½ tsp salt
2 tbsp olive oil
2 tbsp water (if needed)
*50g natural yogurt (we love goats' but
    you can use cows'), to finish*
2 sprigs of mint, to finish

Wash the courgettes and pat dry.
Remove the stem and cut in half lengthways, then cut into 2cm-thick slices. Place in a heavy-bottomed saucepan or large frying pan. Peel the garlic cloves and press each one with the side of the knife to flatten – this helps to release flavour. Add to the courgettes in the pan and sprinkle with the salt and olive oil.

Place the pan on a medium-high heat, cover and set the timer for 8 minutes. After this time, remove the lid and mix well – this will help get the liquids flowing out of the courgette. Reduce the heat to medium and let the courgette and garlic cook down to a mushy pulp, stirring regularly (I like to set a timer every 5 minutes to remind me). You can be vigorous in the stirring, as the end result should be a rough purée. If the courgette begins to stick to the bottom of the pan, use your spoon to scrape up all the lovely flavour. If it is catching too much, reduce the heat slightly and add 2 tablespoons of water. The total cooking time will depend on the water content in the courgettes, but it will take at least 30 minutes (and can take up to 50 minutes) for them to soften entirely.

Remove from the heat and check the seasoning. I find that it doesn't usually need anything more, but you can add a little salt if you wish. You can serve this straight away while it is warm or wait until it has cooled to room temperature. It is best eaten on the day you make it, but will keep well in an airtight container in the fridge for up to a week. Just remember to allow it to come up to room temperature before eating.

Spread the dip on a serving plate – it's nice to use a flat plate – and drizzle all over with the yogurt, so each mouthful will get a bit. Pick the mint leaves and tear them up, then sprinkle over the plate just before serving.

Muhamra

Our floor girls are always experimenting with their diets, always following the latest diet fad, always driving the kitchen crazy with their staff lunch requests ('Is it Tuesday? I can only eat millet today'). When, for a few days in 2013, all of London turned vegan, so did our girls, and they discovered this wonderful dip. They kept on asking for 'just a spoonful' to add to their drab lunches, and have kept on asking even though the vegan period is now behind us. With a name from the Arabic word for 'clay' or 'red', this is our humble take on the Lebanese classic. It has so many good things in it, so much good flavour and such good looks, it will lift any plate, but I find roast chicken or quail to be a particularly good match.

For 4–6 to share as a mezze

1 red pepper (about 180g)
1 large plum tomato (about 120g)
1 red onion (about 100g)
1 head of garlic, unpeeled
1 chilli (red or green)
1 tbsp + 1 tbsp olive oil
½ tsp salt
¼ tsp freshly ground black pepper
60g walnuts, roasted
3 tbsp pomegranate molasses
½ tsp smoky paprika

Preheat your oven to 240°C/220°C fan/ gas mark 9 and line a roasting tin with baking paper.

Quarter the pepper and remove the seeds, then cut each piece into three. Cut the tomato into six wedges. Peel the red onion and cut into six wedges. Hold the head of garlic on its side and cut through the middle so all the cloves are halved and exposed. Place the pepper, tomato, onion, garlic and whole chilli in the roasting pan, drizzle all over with the first tablespoon of olive oil and sprinkle with the salt and pepper. Place the tin in the oven to roast. After 15 minutes carefully open the oven and mix everything well, then roast for a further 15–20 minutes, checking as you go. It will take about 30 minutes in total, as you want the vegetables to start to burn slightly. You may need to give them a little more or less time depending on your oven, but the end result should be strongly caramelised, soft vegetables. Remove from the oven and allow to cool.

Once you can handle the vegetables, squeeze the soft flesh of the garlic cloves out of the skins – it should just pop out, then you can discard the skins. Remove the top stem-part of the chilli. Mix all the vegetables and most of the walnuts together (leave 5–6 walnuts to garnish the top of the dip). Add the pomegranate molasses, the second tablespoon of olive oil and the paprika, then use a food processor or a stick blender to purée to a chunky consistency. It shouldn't be smooth, but it should be brought together to create a paste. Taste and see if you need to add a touch more salt (or, if you like spicy food, you could add a little cayenne or chilli flakes). Transfer to a serving plate and use the reserved walnuts, chopped roughly, as a garnish.

This dip will keep really well for up to a week in an airtight container in the fridge, so you too can add a little lift to your lunches.

Dips, Spreads & Purées.

Baba ganoush – aubergine & tahini dip

The best way ever to roast an aubergine is over charcoal – just put a couple of whole ones on the grill when having a barbecue and turn them occasionally until they are charred and soft. The idea is to get the skin charred and the flesh soft. As we very rarely – if ever – barbecue, we find other solutions to get our fix, as you'll see in the recipe below. Then we use the pulp in so many ways, but this is everyone's favourite.

For 4–6 to share as a mezze

2 small firm aubergines (to yield about 300g pulp)
2 cloves of garlic, peeled
50g tahini paste
2 tbsp lemon juice
¼ tsp salt
fresh pomegranate seeds, to serve (optional)
pomegranate molasses, to serve (optional)

You can use two methods to roast aubergines if you don't happen to have a barbecue handy:

• Option 1: If you have a gas burner, remove the rack and cover the surface under the burner with silver foil. Return the rack and turn on the gas to high heat. Place the aubergines over the direct heat and allow to burn – if you have an extractor fan, turn it on, or open a window. Use a pair of tongs to turn the aubergines, so that they burn all over and feel soft when pressed.

• Option 2: Turn your oven onto the grill setting, or if you have a separate grill use that. Line a tray with aluminium foil or a silicone baking sheet – it's best not to use baking paper as it can burn, but you do want to line the tray as the aubergines leak a sticky liquid that is hard to clean off. Pierce each aubergine twice with the tip of a knife to stop them exploding, and place on the tray directly under the grill. Allow them to burn, then turn (using tongs) and burn again, then turn again... you get the idea.

Once they are completely burnt, transfer them to a plate to cool slightly. When they are cool enough to handle, slit and scoop out all the flesh into a bowl with a spoon. I like to use the liquid that accumulates at the bottom too, as it is full of that wonderful smokiness.

Crush the garlic using a press or a fine grater, then mix with the aubergine pulp, tahini paste, lemon juice and salt. You may want to adjust the level of salt and lemon juice. It is now ready to eat. We like to sprinkle it with a handful of pomegranate seeds and drizzle it with pomegranate molasses, but it works perfectly just as it is.

You can keep the dip for 2–3 days in an airtight container in the fridge, but beware: it may need to be re-seasoned, as both tahini and lemon lose their edge if kept too long.

Labaneh

Labaneh is a strained cheese made by mixing yogurt and lemon juice (plus a little oil and salt) and letting it drain through a cheesecloth or an unworn stocking (I place the stocking inside a tall, narrow vase, folding the top over the sides so it is held in place while I pour the mixture in). The result is like cream cheese but with a much tangier, funkier flavour. It is the first thing I remember making in kindergarten in Israel – it's that easy. You can improve on the basic recipe in so many ways. In the restaurant we like to roll the cheese into small balls, cover them with olive oil, add some oregano sprigs and let them marinate, then serve them on cocktail sticks, like cheesy little bonbons. Sometimes we top them with a sprinkling of za'atar and olive oil. In season we add a handful of wonderful fresh garlic leaves to the basic yogurt-lemon mix. We've suggested below a few more simple variations for flavouring the easiest cheese in the world. You will need to start making it at least a day in advance of serving to give the cheese time to thicken.

Yields about 200g – enough for 4–6 to share as a mezze or about 12 small *labaneh* balls

350g plain yogurt
1 tbsp olive oil
1 tbsp lemon juice
½ tsp salt

Mix everything together, tie it up in a cheesecloth or new stocking and hang it over the sink to drip and drain. I like to leave it at room temperature overnight and then transfer to the fridge in a sieve sitting over a bowl. If you want to serve it as a spread it will be ready the next day – store in an airtight container in the fridge and it will keep well for about a week. If you want to roll it, then best to wait and let it drain for another day or two until all the moisture has dripped out.

The easiest way to make the balls is to rub your hands with a little olive oil, then pick up a small amount of cheese and roll it between your palms – you want to roll each ball to the size of a cherry tomato. Place the balls in a jar or airtight container, cover with a 50:50 mix of olive oil and vegetable oil and add a couple of oregano sprigs. You can add some dried chilli or bay leaves too if you want. Cover and store in the fridge until you want to serve them – *labaneh* balls keep well this way for up to 2 weeks.

Flavour variations to add to the basic yogurt-lemon mix
- ½ teaspoon of nigella seeds and ¼ teaspoon of cracked black pepper
- 1 crushed garlic clove and 3 sprigs of dill, finely chopped
- ½ teaspoon of smoky paprika and 2 tablespoons of sour cream
- use goats' or sheep's yogurt, if you can get some (their particular flavour will really shine through)

Baked
&Fried.

My grandmother's parents came from Egypt and settled in Jerusalem early last century. The extended family lived together in one of those particular Jerusalem homes: built around a courtyard, clad in that particular pinkish-grey Jerusalem stone, overlooking the hills where the Israeli parliament and Supreme Court would later be built, and within walking distance of the market where they made their living.

We were not so much in touch with that side of the family and I know very little about them. They were from Alexandria or Cairo; they came from a lot of money or no money at all; they were originally from Spain, or Aleppo, or Morocco; and there was something a bit 'off' about them (years later a distant cousin was at the centre of a major political scandal; another was or is jailed in Panama – shady stuff). My grandmother lost touch with her brothers, and my mum can barely remember my great-grandparents – only her grandmother's beautiful smile and long grey plaits, and her grandfather sitting in that stone-clad courtyard rolling old newspapers into cones, in which later

he would serve the falafel he sold in the market every weekday from seven in the morning till half past noon.

Years later, after they had both died and the family home was ripped apart in inheritance wars, I went to school not far from their old neighbourhood, and would go on my breaks to the falafel stall that, according to family lore, still uses the same recipe as my great-grandfather did. I am not sure how much truth there is in that, but they are to my mind the best falafel anywhere.

Despite my heritage, it was not I who brought falafel to Honey & Co. I hate frying and would not put anything fried on the menu unless I was sure that someone else was there to fry it. As sometimes happens, my wife takes a different view. And as always happens, she is right – falafel in particular, and fried stuff in general, are what you crave when you sit down to eat: crunchy, greasy, spicy and salty (everything you shouldn't have), with a lot of tahini on top. Keeping this kind of eating to small bites at the start of the meal is the right way to go.

Falafel

Many things are better at room temperature, or cold, or the next day, but falafel is not one of them. Falafel is only splendid if it is eaten as soon as it is fried. When it is all crunchy and hot, you crack it open and the soft fragrant insides are just right. It will hold for 20 minutes or so at room temperature, but really after that it should be discarded. It does not stand reheating well and once cooked should not be refrigerated.

We have placed it here in our mezze section, but of course you can make a meal of it – add a salad and some fresh flatbread and tahini for a winning meal that is enjoyed all over the world, and is my wife's death row dinner.

Preparation is straightforward enough. Falafel always contains chickpeas and onions, and almost always cumin and baking powder, but other than that, anything goes. There are as many variations as there are falafel shops, each with their own recipe and their followers. You may sample and enjoy as many different variations as you like, but your favourite will always be the one across the road from the house you grew up in, the one you'd buy on the way home from school.

Falafel – important things to note before you start

• **You must start all falafel recipes the** night before, or at least 8 hours in advance, by soaking the chickpeas at room temperature in a large bowl with lots of water (it needs to be at least four times the volume of the chickpeas). Falafel will never work with tinned chickpeas – ever.

• **The end weight should be double the** dried weight, so 125g dried chickpeas should end up as 250g soaked.

• **If, when you first cover the chickpeas** with water, it goes murky, strain them and cover with fresh water, as they may be dirty.

• **Once soaked, lift them out of the** water and place in a bowl, rather than tipping the chickpeas and soaking water into a sieve or colander. This way you leave the impurities in the water, rather than tipping them back onto the chickpeas.

• **We suggest you go through them** and remove any chickpeas that have gone

black, along with any little stones you find (it really depends on how well they were packed).

• **You can use a rough meat grinder** attachment or a food processor to mince everything together. We generally favour the meat grinder as it allows for a very evenly-minced result, but ever since we lost our mincer blade we have been using the food processor with very good results.

• **We use gram flour, a chickpea flour** that is really easy to come by nowadays. It makes the recipe gluten-free, but regular flour will work well too.

• **You can prepare the falafel mixture** up to 2 days in advance, as it will keep well in an airtight container in the fridge.

• **Always serve falafel with a tahini dip.** It's just the way it's done – see notes on tahini on page 16.

Jerusalem-style falafel (one for Itamar)

Visitors to the old walled town in Jerusalem entering from the Jaffa gate will be greeted by a blue-painted handcart selling sesame-crusted bread with za'atar to dip, and big torpedo-shaped falafel, a snack for weary tourists. Do not be tempted – these have all been prepared before sunrise and, after hours in the Jerusalem sun, have lost the flavour of their youth. Much better to enter the old town and get lost in the cobbled streets and alleys. You are sure to stumble upon the source, where the bread is fresh out of the oven and the falafel fresh out of the oil. Rich with sesame seeds and fragrant with cinnamon, to me they are the ultimate flavour-fingerprint of this part of the world.

Makes about 14–18 balls (depending on the size you make them)

1 onion, peeled (about 100g)
250g soaked chickpeas
   (from 125g dried – see method on page 92)
1 tsp ground coriander
1 tbsp ground cumin
1 tbsp ground cinnamon
a pinch of white pepper (leave it out rather
   than using black)
¾ tsp salt
2 tbsp gram flour (use plain if need be)
1¼ tsp baking powder
2 tbsp sesame seeds

Haifa-style falafel (one for Sarit)

This is inspired by the flavour of the long-time winner of my personal Haifa falafel competition, which comes from a tiny shop in an alley in Haifa's Wadi Nisnas. The shop's name translates to 'the elders' and they certainly know what they are doing. It is best served with a sharp lemony-type of tahini to cut through the potent cumin and chickpea flavour. This is a recipe for purists, as it offers clear, direct, bold flavours.

1 onion, peeled (about 100g)
1 clove of garlic, peeled
250g soaked chickpeas
   (from 125g dried – see method on page 92)
1 tbsp ground cumin
1 tbsp ground coriander
a pinch of white pepper (leave it out rather
   than using black)
¾ tsp salt
2 tbsp gram flour (use plain flour, if need be)
1 tsp baking powder

Yemeni-style falafel (one for the family roots)

Itamar is a quarter Yemeni on his grandfather's side. This falafel is a tribute to that heritage, and it is great – the traditional Yemeni combo of coriander, cardamom and garlic makes it super-vibrant in colour and flavour.

½ onion, peeled (about 60g)
1 clove of garlic, peeled
250g soaked chickpeas
    (from 125g dried – see note on page 92)
1 green chilli, seeds and all
3 sprigs of parsley, picked
1 small bunch of coriander (about 15–20g),
    leaves and top part of stems only
½ tsp ground cumin
1 tsp freshly ground cardamom pods
½ tsp salt
2 tbsp gram flour (use plain if need be)
1 tsp baking powder

Method if you are using a meat grinder

Use the coarse grinder blade if you have one – we find it gives the best texture. Cut the onion and garlic into dice so that you can easily feed them through the grinder. Mince the chickpeas, onions, garlic,* chilli* and herbs* into a bowl. Add the spices, salt, flour, baking powder and sesame seeds* and mix well to a very thick mass.

* if required by your chosen recipe

Method if you are using a food processor

Start with the onion, garlic,* chilli* and herbs* and pulse them to chop roughly, then add the chickpeas and blitz until everything becomes a thick paste with small, even-sized bits. You may need to scrape the sides down and blitz for another pulse or two to make sure that everything is evenly chopped, but do not overwork. The best way to check whether it is done enough is to scoop up a small amount and squeeze it together in your palm – it should hold its shape. If it falls apart, return it to the processer for another spin. Tip the mixture into a large bowl, add the spices, salt, flour, baking powder and sesame seeds* and mix until all is combined well.

* if required by your chosen recipe

Frying and serving

It is important to fry the falafel in deep oil that will cover them entirely. If you own a fryer, use that. I prefer to fry five at a time in a small pan, rather than waste oil cooking them in a large pan that could hold the entire quantity, but really it is up to you.

Use a neutral vegetable oil that doesn't have much flavour, like sunflower or rapeseed. Heat the pan before adding the falafel. If you want to be scientific about it, or have a fryer with a temperature setting, you are looking for 170°C, or you can test the oil temperature by placing a small piece of bread or falafel mix in the hot oil – as soon as it starts to bubble up and float, you are ready to go.

You can shape the falafel mix in a few different ways: use damp hands and make little balls or torpedo shapes; or you can simply drop in spoonfuls of mixture for free-form falafel. There are special falafel scoops you can buy online if you intend to go pro, but whichever way you choose, you want to be making them about the size of a walnut, no bigger, so that they cook through and crisp up at the same time.

Carefully place the falafel in the oil – don't overcrowd the pan – and fry until the exterior is browned and crisped (about 2–3 minutes). Remove to a plate covered with a paper towel to absorb the excess oil and repeat the process until all them have been fried. Serve right now.

Vegetable fritters

The following recipes make about 25 small fritters, which is enough for 6–8 people as a generous mezze, or for 4 as a vegetarian main course (as we often serve them in the restaurant) with some green salad and a dipping sauce. It seems silly to halve these recipes, as any leftover fritters can be stored in the fridge overnight and will be great the next day in a lunchbox or a sandwich. You can prepare the fritters in advance and warm them up in a medium-hot oven for 5 minutes before serving, but they are also great at room temperature. If you can't be bothered with the dipping sauce, thick natural yogurt is a delicious alternative.

Carrot & butternut fritters

**Serves 6–8
to share as
a mezze**

1 large carrot, peeled (about 150g)
1 medium potato, peeled (about 150g)
¼ butternut squash, peeled and deseeded
    (about 150g)
½ onion, peeled (about 60g)
½ tsp + ½ tsp salt
2 eggs
6 sprigs of tarragon, picked and
    roughly chopped
¼ tsp freshly ground black pepper
½ tsp ground cardamom pods (page 11)
3 tbsp wholemeal flour
½ tsp baking powder
vegetable oil for frying

For the chive sour cream
    1 small tub of sour cream (about 170ml)
    ½ bunch of chives, chopped finely
    1 tsp lemon juice
    1 tbsp mayonnaise
    some freshly ground black pepper

Grate all the vegetables on a coarse grater (or use a food processor) and place in a sieve over a bowl. Sprinkle with half a teaspoon of salt and mix lightly. Allow to sit for at least 30 minutes at room temperature to draw out the excess water.

Place the eggs, tarragon, remaining half-teaspoon of salt, pepper, ground cardamom, flour and baking powder in a bowl. Squeeze out whatever liquid you can from the vegetables, add them to the bowl and mix vigorously to combine.

Heat about 2cm of oil in a frying pan, and line a plate with some absorbent kitchen paper. Scoop little spoonfuls of the batter into the oil and fry for about a minute until they start to crisp up. Flip the fritters carefully and fry on the other side for another minute or so till crisp. Remove to the lined plate to absorb the excess oil. Repeat until you have used up all the batter.

Mix all the chive sour cream ingredients together (I wouldn't add any salt, as chives have a natural saltiness to them) and serve with the fritters.

Courgette & herb fritters

1 small potato, peeled (about 150g)
½ onion, peeled (about 60g)
1 clove of garlic, peeled
2 small green courgettes, trimmed
  (about 300g)
1 tsp salt
2 eggs
3 sprigs of mint, picked and coarsely chopped
5 sprigs of parsley, picked and
  coarsely chopped
a pinch of freshly ground black pepper
50g self-raising flour
vegetable oil for frying

For the garlic yogurt
  100g natural yogurt
  1 clove of garlic, peeled and crushed
  1 tbsp olive oil
  1 tsp lemon juice
  a touch of salt
  some freshly ground black pepper

Grate the potato, onion, garlic and courgettes on a coarse grater (you can use a food processor) and place in a sieve over a bowl. Sprinkle the salt over the vegetables and mix lightly. Allow to sit for at least 30 minutes at room temperature.

Put the eggs, herbs and black pepper in a mixing bowl. Squeeze out any excess liquid from the vegetables and add them to the bowl, then sprinkle with the flour and mix together to a thick paste.

Heat about 2cm of oil in a frying pan to shallow-fry the fritters, and cover a plate with some absorbent kitchen paper. Drop little spoonfuls of the batter into the oil and fry for about 2 minutes, until they start to go golden at the edges. Flip the fritters carefully and fry on the other side till golden. Remove to the lined plate to absorb any excess oil. Repeat until you have used up all the batter.

Mix all the garlic yogurt ingredients together until smooth and serve alongside the fritters.

Feta & spring onion bouikos

Most mornings in our kitchen, this happens:

Our pastry chef Giorgia (*heavy Italian accent, angry*):
> Sarit! Tell your husband to stop eat my *bouikos*!

Itamar (*Israeli accent, full mouth*):
> I can eat what I want! Everything here is mine! It's my restaurant!

Giorgia (*angrier, grabs a rolling pin*):
> The restaurant is yours; the pastry is mine!

Itamar (*reaches for another* bouikos):
> Remember who signs your pay cheque!

Giorgia (*bashes his hand with said rolling pin*):
> Sarit signs my pay cheque! Go #¡≈†€∞$£@ (*Italian swear words*)!

Itamar: %*§¢#¡£@≈† (*swear words in Hebrew*) Cosa Nostra! £@€*§¢#¡∞ (*more swear words in Hebrew*)!

Bouikos are little cheese buns from the Balkans. We have had them in our mezze selection almost since day one. They are lovely at room temperature but once you've tried them fresh from the oven, you'll see why it is worth invoking the wrath of the Mafia.

Makes 12 small or 6 large

50g cold butter
40g mature Cheddar cheese
40g feta
100g plain flour
a pinch of salt
50ml sour cream
½ tsp nigella seeds
2 spring onions, chopped
   (or 2 tbsp chopped chives)
milk to glaze (optional)

There are two key factors in getting the best texture here: use cold ingredients and work them as little as possible. Cut your cold butter into small cubes the size of playing dice. Grate the Cheddar cheese and crumble the feta, then combine all the ingredients together straight away. You can use a mixer with a paddle attachment or just your hands. Work the mixture until it just combines; lumps of butter and cheese are exactly what you want in this dough – when you bake it, they will melt and ooze and be so tasty.

Place the dough on a lightly floured surface and pat it down to a rough rectangle about 2–3cm thick (roughly the same height as the first joint of your thumb). I traditionally cut it into triangles like this – flour the blade of your knife, cut the dough in half lengthways, slice across three times to divide it into six squares, then cut each of these from corner to corner to give you twelve small triangles. You can also make squares, rounds or rectangles (if you choose to go with rounds, you will need to re-form the offcuts by pushing them together and patting down, so that you use up all the dough). If you want to freeze any for future use, now is the time – lay the dough shapes on a flat tray with a little space between each one and place in the freezer. Once they are fully frozen you can pack them in a container or freezer bag. Just thaw at room temperature for 30–60 minutes before baking. ›››

Preheat your oven to 220°C/200°C fan/gas mark 7.

You can brush the top with a little milk if you want them to be shiny, but it isn't vital for the flavour. Bake on a lined baking tray on the upper-middle shelf of the oven for 10 minutes. Open the oven and carefully turn the tray round, then reduce the temperature to 200°C/180°C fan/gas mark 6 and bake for a further 6–8 minutes until they are golden.

You can eat these straight away, or you can cool them on the tray until you are ready to serve. They are best eaten the same day.

Variations
You can vary the flavours if you wish: instead of using spring onion and nigella seeds you could substitute:
- ½ teaspoon of smoky paprika and a pinch of chilli flakes; or
- ½ teaspoon of freshly ground black pepper and the leaves from 2 sprigs of thyme.

Borekitas

It took us months to get these just right, but we are so pleased with the result, as they are truly gorgeous. The star here is the pastry. It is known in our kitchen as 'dough number 4' – the number assigned to it in the final session of blind tasting, where it was the clear, unanimous winner. The cold, finely diced butter gives it a lovely flake and the double cream adds a richness that makes it nearly impossible to resist having another one. There are enough alternative fillings to make a cookbook on their own – burnt aubergine, potato, mushroom, merguez sausage... the list goes on – but this spinach and cheese filling is a good place to start, and also to stop, if you so wish.

Makes about 20

For the pastry dough
  150g cold butter, diced and chilled
  150ml double cream
  a pinch of salt
  a pinch of sugar
  300g plain flour
  1 egg yolk

For the filling
  100g baby spinach, washed
  1 egg
  40g feta, crumbled
  40g kashkaval cheese, grated
    (or use pecorino)
  2 tbsp chopped dill
  3 sprigs of thyme, picked

beaten egg or milk, to glaze
sesame, nigella or poppy seeds,
  to decorate (optional)

Put all the ingredients for the dough in a large bowl and use the tips of your fingers to bring together (or use a mixer with a paddle attachment). You want small flecks of butter to remain visible – when you come to bake the pastry dough, they will melt and fluff it up to a buttery goodness. Form the dough into a ball, wrap in cling film and rest it in the fridge for at least 1 hour. You can prepare the dough up to 2 days in advance of baking – just keep it wrapped in cling film in the fridge until you need it.

Wilt the spinach in a pan over a high heat – after 1–2 minutes it should have lost its shape but not its colour. Quickly remove to a colander to drain. Mix the other filling ingredients together in a bowl. Once the spinach has cooled down a little, press it with the back of a spoon to squeeze out any excess liquid, then remove from the colander and chop roughly. Stir the spinach into the filling mixture and season to taste with salt (but remember that the cheese is salty, so don't go overboard) and a generous helping of black pepper.

Preheat your oven to 200°C/180°C fan/gas mark 6. ›››

Flour your work surface and roll the dough out as thinly as possible. I like to use an 8cm round cutter to make disk shapes, but you can use a wine glass, or cut the dough into squares if you prefer. Place the dough shapes on a lined baking tray as you go. Re-roll any scraps so that you can keep cutting out shapes, but be aware that the more times you roll it, the less flaky it will be. I discard any leftover pastry dough after rolling it out three times.

Pop a teaspoon of filling in the centre of each disk (or square) and fold the dough over so that the filling is covered. Use your fingers to pinch the edges of the dough together tightly to seal. If you want to freeze any to bake another day, this is the time to do so – lay the filled pastries on a flat tray with a little space between each one and place in the freezer. Once they are fully frozen you can pack them in a container or freezer bag. They will keep like this for up to a month. All you need to do is take them out of the freezer to thaw at room temperature for an hour before baking.

Brush the *borekitas* with beaten egg or milk to glaze and sprinkle them with a few seeds (if using – they are more for the look than the flavour). Bake in the centre of the oven for 15–20 minutes or until golden. These are best served warm and eaten on the day of baking.

Cracked.

When posting an advert for a kitchen porter you may get hundreds of applications. You can't go through them all; you need to have a system. I always go by the best-sounding name. This is how I came to invite Hernan David Geitzinger for an interview. I could not imagine what a guy with such a name would even look like. It turned out that he looked like a short, thin 12-year-old boy, though he was 26 at the time. The work is hard, I explained to him, plenty of running and heavy lifting; I don't think it's for you. But he asked to do a trial shift, so he got to do a trial shift, and after two hours he was offered a job. We named him HD for short, and he turned out to be not only a terrific kitchen porter but also a natural-born leader. He quickly moved from porter to prep, from prep to chef and is now one of the best chefs (and one of the best people) I know.

I stayed with the name system, and we found ourselves with Marcus Aurelius, an energetic Spaniard whom everyone liked at first – he was fast and clean, paid attention and improved, and was very charismatic. That lasted for about a week. Then he started coming late to work; things didn't get done; the kitchen was not clean. I sat him down for a 'do or die' talk. He improved for two days and then on the Friday he didn't show up for work and didn't call. We never saw him again. On Saturday, our busiest day of the week, we came to work to find the door had been broken and there was a big crack in the window. There was no mess, nothing else broken, but the laptop with all our accounts on it and a cashbox with the

previous day's takings had gone. That Saturday could have been complete chaos – without a computer, with all the bookings delayed – but everyone was really nice once we explained, and really supportive. By the end of the day we had a new door and a new computer, and though it took us weeks to recover all the data we had lost on the laptop, we got there eventually. We kept the crack in the window, though we could have had it mended for a song. It is a strange reminder every time we walk in, although I'm not sure what of – that everything can go wrong in a minute, or perhaps that things will always go wrong and then bounce back, or maybe simply that we need to back up our computer. I have stuck with the name system though. Our porters now are called Pierre Paolo Racis, Danielle Pistouz and – the best of all – Dawid Isajew (he isn't).

Bulgar or cracked wheat has been a staple at the restaurant from the beginning. It is served as a side order for those who want to soak up the juice of a slow-cooked dish, and is almost always on our menu as a salad, either in the mezze selection or as a bed for chicken to rest upon. We prefer it to couscous as it has more texture and flavour but is just as easy to prepare. There are different grades available and, as with everything else, we don't agree on which is best. We settled on a medium grind for the restaurant and for most of the recipes in this book, but we have tried them with a coarse grind too and they work well with only a slight adjustment when cooking the wheat (it needs a bit more water than the medium grind).

Basic bulgar wheat

For every 75g of bulgar wheat you will need a pinch of salt, a splash of olive oil and 75ml of boiling water (90ml for coarse grind). Place the bulgar wheat, oil and salt in a bowl and stir well till the grains are all coated in the oil. Pour over just-boiled water and quickly cling film the bowl to seal in the steam. Leave for 5 minutes and then carefully uncover. Use a fork or a small whisk to fluff the bulgar wheat up and break the mass into individual grains (or rub it between your palms to break it up). Allow to cool uncovered and then it is ready to use. It will keep like this for 3 days in an airtight container in the fridge.

75g of dried will make 150g of cooked bulgar wheat. This is the amount we use in most of the following recipes, each of which should be enough for 4–6 as part of a mezze selection. As these salads are all about freshness, at the restaurant we make a new batch for each service and only serve them that day. That said, whenever we have some left over, we eat it as staff lunch with tahini or yogurt the following day, and no one complains.

Tomato & pomegranate tabule for high summer

This is best made when tomatoes are in high season and are sweet and full of flavour. Use coarse grind bulgar wheat for this, as the soft tomatoes need the added crunch.

100g cooked coarse grind bulgar wheat
   (see method above)
100g fresh pomegranate seeds
100g tomatoes, cut into small dice
1 large bunch of parsley (about 30–40g),
   picked and chopped
3 sprigs of mint, picked and chopped
1 green chilli, deseeded and chopped
2 inner stalks of celery, finely sliced
zest and juice of 1 lemon
1 tbsp olive oil
½ tsp sea salt

Mix everything together in a bowl and adjust the seasoning to taste. Eat straight away.

Apricot & pistachio tabule with orange blossom

This one is autumnal in flavour, colour and feel, but as it relies on store cupboard ingredients, we enjoy it all year round.

80g roasted pistachios, coarsely chopped
150g cooked bulgar wheat
   (see method on page 108)
120g dried apricots, cut into strips
   (we use scissors)
1 tbsp orange blossom water
zest and juice of 1 orange
1 tbsp lemon juice (about ½ lemon)
3–4 sprigs of parsley, picked and
   coarsely chopped
3–4 sprigs of mint, picked and
   coarsely chopped
1 tbsp olive oil, plus a little for drizzling
a pinch of salt to taste
   (only if you feel it is lacking)

Set aside 30g of the chopped pistachios – you will use them later to sprinkle on top. Place the rest of the pistachios and all the other ingredients apart from the salt in a bowl. Mix well and taste, adding the salt if you feel it needs it. This dish can be prepared a few hours in advance of eating, but is best kept out of the fridge in the meantime, as chilling would affect the flavour significantly and you would have to re-season before serving.

Transfer to a serving bowl and sprinkle with the remaining pistachios just before serving, to keep them crunchy.

Cracked.

Crunchy root vegetable tabule for winter

A great solution for the cold months when the shops are full of lovely roots and you crave something light, fresh and brightly-flavoured after weeks of eating cooked winter dishes.

1 lemon
3 tbsp olive oil
2 tsp za'atar, plus 1 tsp for garnish
¼ head of celeriac, peeled (about 100g)
1 carrot, peeled (about 50g)
1 small bunch of radishes (about 100g)
4–5 sprigs of parsley, picked
150g cooked bulgar wheat
   (see method on page 108)

To make the dressing, zest the lemon and then juice it. Mix with the olive oil and 2 teaspoons of za'atar. Season to taste with salt and pepper.

Cut the celeriac and carrot into thin matchsticks. This is really easy to do using one of those vegetable peelers with teeth that seem to be available everywhere now – you just run the peeler over it and you are ready to go. Alternatively do it the old-fashioned way – slowly with a knife. Slice the radish thinly into rounds. Mix the celeriac, carrot, radish and parsley leaves together in a bowl. You can prepare this a few hours in advance and store it in the fridge until needed.

When you are ready to serve, add the cooked bulgar wheat and the dressing to the vegetables and stir to combine. Transfer to a serving dish and sprinkle with the remaining za'atar. Serve straight away.

Cracked.

Green tabule salad for spring

This is the closest to original tabule salad. The dominant flavours are herby and green, and the taste of the olive oil should really shine through, so use the good stuff here.

1 Lebanese cucumber or ½ regular cucumber
(about 150g)
2 spring onions, finely chopped
70g cooked bulgar wheat
(see method on page 108;
use 35g raw weight)
1 bunch of parsley, roughly chopped
(about 15–20g)
4 sprigs of mint, picked and chopped (2 tbsp)
½ tsp salt
2 tbsp best quality olive oil
juice of ½–1 lemon (1–2 tbsp)

Mix everything together as close to eating as possible for the best flavour and to stop it going soggy. I recommend that you just add the juice of half the lemon to begin with and taste to see what you think. We love this sharp and would always add more lemon, but you may find that this is enough for you.

I like to keep the skin on the cucumber, and if you can get hold of a Lebanese one, you can chop the whole thing into dice (as small as you can). If you can only get a European long cucumber, it is best to halve it lengthways then scoop out the seeds with a teaspoon and discard before dicing, as otherwise they make the salad too wet.

Couscous & chickpeas in ras el hanut spice

Bland couscous usually gets its flavour from a strong broth – it soaks up all the juices from the meat and vegetables and it becomes a meal. This recipe is a bit of a short cut as the flavour is already in the couscous, so it needs nothing else. It also makes a great store cupboard supper if you use normally-forbidden tinned chickpeas.

Enough for 6–8 as part of a mezze selection, or 2 as a light supper

½ small onion, peeled and finely chopped (about 60g)
3 cloves of garlic, peeled and thinly sliced
1 tbsp olive oil
1 tsp salt
1 tbsp ras el hanut spice mix
100g cooked chickpeas (from 40g dried – see method on page 92; or used tinned)
1 tomato, diced
60g couscous
180ml boiling water
1 small bunch of coriander, chopped (about 15–20g)

Fry the onion and garlic with the oil in a frying pan on a medium heat for about 5 minutes until they get a little colour and soften. Add the salt and ras el hanut and mix well for about 20 seconds to release the flavours. Tip in the chickpeas and tomato dice and cook for a further minute. Add the couscous and boiling water, bring to the boil, then turn the heat off and cover. Allow the couscous to absorb the liquid for 10 minutes, then remove the lid and use a fork to loosen the mass and mix in the chopped coriander. It is now ready to serve.

If we are eating this as a light supper, we like to fry or poach an egg and pop it on top, allowing the yolk to ooze into the couscous. Alternatively you could serve this alongside a piece of grilled chicken or fish.

Kisir

This Turkish canapé is made usually with the hot red pepper paste that is very common there and hard to find here. We fake it with a mixture of tomato purée, chilli, paprika and pimento (allspice) to good effect, but if you can get your hands on *acı biber salçası* (ideally from a market in Istanbul), buy it and try this recipe with it instead. We like to serve this wetter version of bulgar salad in small boats of Little Gem lettuce. They add a crisp freshness and are an easy way to serve this as a pre-dinner nibble at a dinner party. If you do this, get some pomegranate seeds to sprinkle over the top.

This makes enough filling for 16–20 small leaves – perfect party food

½ small onion, peeled and finely chopped
  (about 60g)
1 clove of garlic, peeled and crushed
1 tbsp olive oil
2 tsp paprika
½ tsp ground pimento (allspice)
½ tsp chilli flakes
½ tsp salt
60g bulgar wheat
2 tbsp tomato purée
2 tbsp pomegranate molasses
240ml boiling water
50g roasted walnuts, roughly chopped
1–2 heads of Little Gem lettuce,
  whole leaves separated and washed

Fry the onion and garlic with the oil in a frying pan on a medium heat until they are soft but not coloured (about 4–5 minutes). Sprinkle in the dried spices and salt and mix well for 30 seconds, moving everything around all the time to avoid burning. Then add the bulgar wheat, tomato purée and molasses, and stir to coat thoroughly. Now pour in the boiling water. Be careful – it will spit. Stir once, then turn off the heat and cover the pan.

Allow to rest for 10 minutes, then uncover, add the roasted walnuts and mix through a little. Re-cover and keep covered until you are ready to fill each little lettuce leaf with a heaped tablespoonful of the mixture. This will keep, covered, at room temperature for a few hours before serving – don't refrigerate it, as the cold will affect the flavour and texture.

Cracked.

Fresh
Salads.

Bonnie, a lively 20-year-old, worked with us in our previous job. We both liked her immediately and for some reason felt a bit protective towards her, maybe because she is such a tiny creature. She was a waitress but wanted to study organic agriculture or something like that, and was looking for some hands-on farm experience. She got to hear of a school in northern Israel that had an organic farm and exchanged some emails with them to arrange a work placement. As a South African girl educated in liberal private schools, she was unprepared for the Israeli play-it-by-ear attitude to life. I think she expected that some sort of learning programme would have been prepared for her and her fellow volunteers; the reality was that the school had forgotten she was coming and had no idea what to do with her. She spent her first few nights in the school building, on a mattress in the gym, then someone remembered there was a disused bomb shelter at the edge of the village where she would have running water and a window overlooking the valley. With no one to guide her, she made her own curriculum: she just followed people around and offered to lend a hand – in the cowsheds, in the orchards, with the goats. She decided to attach herself to a group of teens who arrived in a bus every morning to work the fields. It was high summer; they were picking cucumbers, watermelons and tomatoes, and though no one spoke any English she made friends. When one of the girls invited her out with them, Bonnie tried to get on the bus. The field manager ran up to her and eventually managed to explain that her new friend, and all the others for that matter, were mental patients – very sick – from a hospital nearby and this was part of their treatment.

We were in Israel on holiday and wanted to surprise her. She was easy to find: everyone in the village knew her. We were a bit alarmed when we saw her – already a tiny thing before she left the UK, she was even skinnier now. Without a kitchen and with no money, she was living only on fruit and veg from the fields and had not had a cooked meal in weeks. As if to prove to us how well she was blending in, she prepared the ubiquitous spread of the Israeli summer – watermelon that was as big as her and as sweet, and salty cheese from the dairy.

The more she told us of her misadventures – getting lost in the valley, hiking in the desert – the more concerned we became, but she was brown from the sun and as happy as could be, doing exactly what you should do when you are 20. Organic farming was not for her, thank goodness, nor was garden design, or any of the other things she dabbled with. She is now a chef with plenty of talent and motivation. She is working with us at Honey & Co, where we can keep a close eye on her – or at least make sure she gets a cooked meal every now and then.

'Recipes' is too grand a term for the preparations in this chapter. These are simple assemblies of one ingredient in its prime with some things to complement it. They won't take long to prepare and are extremely satisfying to eat; they are tasty and light, feel virtuous and are quite easy on the eye to boot. Some combinations are old and traditional, like watermelon and feta, or beetroots and walnuts; others just make so much sense that they are almost food clichés. But all these dishes depend on getting the right main ingredient at the right time and treating it in the right way.

Most of the recipes in this chapter will give you four starter portions or two main-sized ones, or enough for six to eight as part of a mezze selection. You can serve them on a large platter for everyone to share, or on individual plates if you don't trust the people you feed to share nicely.

Fig, goats' cheese & honey salad

We used to make this salad with honey from Regent's Park, which is 5 minutes' walk from the restaurant. Toby, the beekeeper, would deliver it to us on his push bike. He once brought his bees – 'the girls' – with him, which caused more panic than joy, though they were perfectly well-behaved. Honey is one of those ingredients, like wine, that gives a flavour-snapshot of the place it comes from, and this honey tasted of mint and grass. Even though it was eye-wateringly expensive, we used it for everything, and it was worth it. Toby is now in San Francisco. We aren't sure who is looking after his 'girls' but we enjoy playing with different kinds of honey. In this recipe we use thyme honey but you can use other types. Look for one that is light and fragrant rather than heady or rich, which would overpower the dish. We use a log of British goats' cheese and remove the rind, but you could use a softer, rindless variety if you prefer.

Serves 3–4 as a light starter

2 heads of Little Gem lettuce
8 large figs (or 12 small ones), quartered
3 sprigs of fresh mint, picked
50g roasted pistachios, roughly chopped
sea salt
freshly ground black pepper
2 tbsp olive oil
juice of ½ lemon
2 tsp thyme honey

For the goats' cheese
120g goats' cheese
zest of ½ lemon
3 tbsp double cream

Separate the lettuce leaves and wash in cold water. Cut the large leaves in half but keep the small inner ones whole. Dry on a few sheets of kitchen paper or in a salad spinner.

Crumble the goats' cheese into the bowl of a food processor and mix with the lemon zest and cream until completely smooth and airy. Alternatively, you could whisk by hand.

Arrange the lettuce leaves on a large serving platter and scatter over the fig wedges and mint leaves. Top with the chopped pistachios and dollops of the creamy goats' cheese. Sprinkle with salt and pepper and follow with the oil and lemon juice. Finish by drizzling the honey all over the salad.

Tomato & za'atar fatoush

In our first week of trade a tall redhead in a long (fake) fur coat walked in, looked at the menu, asked loads of questions and ordered some food. She came back with her father, then with the boyfriend, then with some girlfriends, and each time ordered some more. Kim became a friend and this salad became her favourite. We made it for her birthday in March, as it works just as well with crunchy green winter tomatoes as it does with ripe red ones.

Serves 4 as a starter or 2 as a main

1 pitta (page 56), cut in half to make two thin round pieces (not two thick half-moons!)
olive oil
1 head of Little Gem lettuce
250g mixed tomatoes
150g feta
2 sprigs of fresh oregano, picked
2 tsp za'atar
2 heaped tbsp fresh pomegranate seeds

For the dressing
1 clove of garlic
2 tbsp good olive oil (this salad is worth it)
1 tbsp red wine vinegar (we use a Corinthian one)
¼ tsp sea salt
a pinch of black pepper

Peel the garlic and place it on a chopping board, then press down on it with the side of a knife until it is crushed but stays in one piece. Mix it together with the other dressing ingredients and allow to infuse for at least an hour at room temperature. Remove the garlic just before mixing the dressing with the salad; it is only there to give a slight hint of flavour that works well with the tomatoes.

Brush the pitta pieces with a little oil and toast them until they're lightly golden and crispy. You can grill them or use your toaster – just watch that they don't burn. Break into bite-sized shards, but make sure they're not too small.

Separate the lettuce into leaves and wash in cold water. Dry on a few sheets of kitchen paper or in a salad spinner. Cut the leaves into large strips.

Cut the tomatoes in two or three different ways (slices, wedges, chunks, dice) to give the salad some texture. The pieces should all be roughly bite-sized – not too small or they will become watery. Break the feta into chunks but try not to crumble it to a paste. All these preparations can be done up to an hour in advance.

When you are ready to serve, remove the garlic clove from the dressing. Take a large bowl, place the pitta shards, lettuce, tomatoes, feta, oregano and za'atar in it, pour the dressing over and mix together. Serve on a large platter or individual plates and top with the pomegranate seeds.

Beetroot & plums in a rose & walnut dressing

Both plums and beets are available in so many shapes and colours that this salad has a lot of possible combinations: pink beets and green plums; yellow beets and purple plums; purple beets and yellow plums. They all work – very disco and delicious.

Serves 4 as a starter or 2 as a main

50g salt
750g beetroots (you will end up with about 400g prepped)
2 sprigs of fresh oregano, picked
1 tbsp red wine vinegar
1 tbsp olive oil
1 small bag of rocket leaves (about 55g), washed
4 sprigs of mint
4 plums

For the walnut dressing
60g freshly roasted walnuts
1 tbsp rose water
1 tsp honey
1 tbsp olive oil
¼ tsp freshly ground black pepper

Heat your oven to 220°C/200°C fan/ gas mark 7. Spread aluminium foil over a baking tray and sprinkle with the salt, then place the beetroots (whole with their skins still on) on top of the salt and place in the centre of the oven to roast for about 1½–2 hours, depending on size. The salt absorbs any moisture in the oven, helping the beets to roast rather than poach. This will result in sweet flavourful beetroot, so don't be tempted to skip this stage and buy ready-cooked – it won't be the same. To check if the beets are done, just insert a small knife into the largest one; it should slide in and out without resistance.

Remove the beets from the oven and allow to cool to a temperature you can handle, then take them off the tray and put on a chopping board. Discard the salt. If you have disposable gloves, I suggest you use them now. With a small knife remove the stalks and peel the beets. Cut into bite-sized wedges. Adjust the size of the wedges as necessary – if your beets are huge, halve them before cutting, or keep them whole if they are small. If you are using more than one colour, it's nice also to vary the shape, so you could cube the yellow or pink ones.

Place the beetroot pieces in a bowl (or two separate bowls if you are using different coloured ones, as otherwise the red ones will stain the rest and it will be a wasted effort). Add the oregano leaves, vinegar and olive oil and mix well. The beets will be so tasty at this stage that you'll want to eat them all, but wait – these beets are going places. This preparation can be done up to a day in advance; just cover and refrigerate the beets until you need them.

Roughly chop the freshly roasted walnuts. Place in a small bowl, add the remaining dressing ingredients and mix well.

To serve, place the rocket and mint leaves on a large platter or individual plates and scatter the beetroot all over. Cut each plum into eight wedges and add them too. You can season very lightly with sea salt at this stage, but make sure to taste the beets before you do as they get a fair amount of salt from the roasting, so they may not need any more. Then generously spoon over all the walnut dressing and serve immediately – you have waited long enough.

Artichokes & kashkaval with pine nuts

With this romantic vegetable you start with a flower and, after a lot of hard and painful work, you end up with a stripped naked heart. It is not worth making for just anyone, so choose your dining companion with care.

Serves 4 as a starter or 2 as a main

½ small red onion, peeled and very finely chopped (about 60g)
60ml white wine vinegar
4 large canned artichokes (page 46) – store-bought will not work here; you have to make them yourself
1 large bag of lamb's lettuce or baby spinach (about 100g), washed
50g roasted pine nuts
a pinch of sea salt
freshly ground black pepper, to taste
50g kashkaval cheese (or pecorino if you can't find it)

Start by mixing the chopped onion with the vinegar and leave to infuse for about 20 minutes.

Cut the artichokes into wedges and place in a small pan with some of their cooking oil on a medium heat to warm up (you can do this in the microwave for 1–2 minutes if you prefer).

Lay the lettuce or spinach leaves on a serving platter as a bed for the warm artichoke wedges to rest upon and sprinkle with the pine nuts, salt and pepper. Using a peeler, shave the cheese all over the platter in long thin slivers, then spoon the vinegar and onion mixture over everything, along with a couple of teaspoons of the artichoke cooking oil. Serve quickly before the leaves start to wilt.

Jerusalem water salad

This is somewhere between a salad and a cold soup – chopped vegetables dressed with cold water that takes on their flavour. It was originally made by the poor households of Jerusalem, where even a tablespoon of oil was a luxury, and continued to be made as the city became more affluent because it is such a good dish. Prepare this only in high summer, when tomatoes and cucumbers are at their best, and serve it when you're in need of a fresh and reviving starter to a heavier main, or as a virtuous meal with a bit of bread.

Serves 4 as a starter

1 Lebanese cucumber or ½ regular cucumber, peeled (about 150g)
2 spring onions
1 red pepper (or ½ yellow and ½ red) (about 100g)
1 handful of small radishes (about 50g)
2 tomatoes, seeds removed (about 150g)
1 clove of garlic, peeled
juice of ½ lemon
240ml water
½ tsp salt
a pinch of freshly ground black pepper

Dice the cucumber, spring onions, pepper, radishes and tomatoes as small as you possibly can, mince or crush the garlic clove and mix them all together in a bowl. Cover and chill in the fridge until you are ready to serve, but not for more than a few hours.

Just before serving, add the lemon juice, water, salt and pepper and mix well. Serve in little bowls and eat with spoons.

Spring salad

It is best to make this salad in the spring, as the name suggests, when you can buy fresh pods of peas and broad beans that have superior flavour and texture. You will need to buy a much larger amount in the pod – about 250g of beans and 150g of peas – as the edible bits only make up a small part of the total weight (about 30% for broad beans and 50% for peas). At other times of the year ignore this advice and use the frozen stuff – it'll feel like May. At the restaurant we use Manouri cheese, an obscure Greek number that is, sadly, really hard to come by, but Halloumi makes a terrific alternative.

Serves 4 as a starter or 2 as a main

70g shelled peas
70g shelled broad beans
1 litre water
1 tsp table salt
1 head of Little Gem lettuce
1 courgette
3 sprigs of fresh mint, picked
a pinch of sea salt
a pinch of freshly ground black pepper
juice of ½ lemon
2 tbsp olive oil, plus 1 tsp for frying
240g Manouri or Halloumi cheese

For the lemon sauce
   1 tbsp olive oil
   1 small unwaxed lemon (about 80g), finely
      sliced, skin and all, seeds removed
   a pinch of saffron (or turmeric,
      if you prefer)
   100ml water, plus more if needed
   1 tsp honey

First make the lemon sauce. Heat the oil in a small frying pan and add the lemon slices. Toss them around and cook for 2–3 minutes until they start to colour. Add the saffron (or turmeric) and water and bring to the boil, then reduce the heat as low as it will go and cook slowly for about 30 minutes. You may need to add a little more water. Once the lemons are very soft, stir in the honey and mix well. Transfer to a food processor or use a hand-held stick blender to purée until completely smooth.

Bring the water and salt to a rapid boil. Plunge the peas for 30 seconds (10 if you're using frozen) then remove with a slotted spoon to a bowl of iced water. Return the water to the boil and repeat the process with the broad beans. They will need 1 minute in the water (30 seconds if they are frozen). Remove the peas and beans from the ice as soon as they're cold, to avoid them getting waterlogged. If you want to, you can remove the outer skin from the broad beans by pinching them and squeezing out the beans, but it's OK not to.

Separate the lettuce into leaves, then wash and dry them. Cut the large leaves in half but keep the small inner ones whole.

Use a vegetable peeler to create thin ribbons of courgette. Mix in a large bowl with the peas, broad beans, lettuce, mint leaves, sea salt, pepper, lemon juice and oil. Then arrange on a large platter or individual serving plates.

Cut the cheese into eight thick slices. Heat a teaspoon of oil in a frying pan on a medium-high heat and cook the cheese for about 30 seconds, then flip the slices over to cook on the other side for another 30 seconds. They should get a nice golden crust.

Place a couple of slices on each individual salad or arrange them over the large serving platter. Dot the lemon sauce over the salad, making sure to get some on each slice of cheese. Serve immediately.

Watermelon & feta

When it's too hot to eat, you want to sit on your balcony hoping for some breeze, have a cold bit of watermelon (to quench the thirst as much as the hunger) and alternate with a bit of salty cheese. This combination may sound strange but is commonplace in the Middle East and the Balkans, and in a way is not so different from the more familiar melon and ham combo: sweet and juicy meets dry and salty.

Serves 4–6 as a starter

¼ fresh watermelon (or you could use one
   of the baby ones that can be found in large
   supermarkets)
½ green chilli
2 tbsp olive oil
1 tbsp lemon juice (about ½ lemon)
1–2 heads of Little Gem lettuce
150g feta
4 sprigs of fresh oregano
sea salt
freshly ground black pepper

Cut the watermelon flesh away from the skin and chop into large cubes. Don't worry about making them exactly square; they just need to be a size that can be lifted with a fork and shoved in your mouth easily. Put the watermelon in the fridge and keep it there until the last minute as it needs to be eaten cold.

Slice the chilli really finely – we leave the seeds in, but if you prefer a more mellow kick, shake them out. Place in a small bowl or jug and cover with the olive oil and lemon juice. Set aside until serving.

Pull the lettuce apart and wash the leaves in cold water. Drain or dry in a salad spinner. We like to keep the leaves whole for this and use them to line a large serving platter. Scatter the watermelon over the lettuce, then break the feta up into chunks (about half the size of the watermelon cubes) and dot them all over. Pick the leaves off the oregano sprigs and scatter them over the top. Finally, just before serving, sprinkle everything with salt and pepper and spoon over the chilli oil. Serve immediately.

Big Itzik

The idea behind this dish is simple but winning – burn and chop a whole bunch of vegetables, add some herbs and seasoning, then mix just enough to leave it somewhere between a salad and a dip. I think this particular version is Turkish, as we've had similar things in Istanbul, but we first had it in a kebab shop run by a huge guy called Big Itzik. The shop was tucked behind a taxi rank in a smelly alley in Jaffa and so we always associate these flavours with the reek of cheap diesel fumes. As is the custom in those parts, while we waited for our meat to cook, our table would be piled up with salads of quality and freshness, and this one always stood out from the crowd. This salad and the grilled sweetbreads were what kept us going back there. And knowing we could always get a taxi back home. This salad is all about the method, as there is hardly any added seasoning; the flavour is in the charring of the vegetables. They develop a slight smokiness and the heat caramelises their sugar content. If you aren't cooking outside your house will become very smoky indeed, but good things come at a price.

Serves 4–6 as a starter with some bread

1 red onion
2 aubergines
1 red pepper
1 yellow or orange pepper (or another red one, but not green)
1 tbsp lemon juice
1 tbsp white wine vinegar
1 large clove of garlic, peeled and finely chopped
2 tbsp chopped parsley
8–10 mint leaves, ripped in half
a sprinkle of sea salt, plus more to taste
1 tbsp olive oil

Now, the absolute ideal would be to use a BBQ for this, but if that isn't a possibility, use a gas hob. Cover the surface of the hob with aluminium foil and turn the largest gas burner on. Place the onion (skin and all) in the centre, and put the whole aubergines and peppers around it, touching the flame directly.

Allow the vegetables to burn fully on one side before rotating them using tongs. The whole charring process should take about 25–35 minutes and by the end the vegetables should be entirely blackened. The peppers will be ready first; when the flesh softens and the skin is all charred remove them to a bowl and cover with clingfilm. The aubergines are ready when they lose their shape and collapse – this means the flesh is fully cooked. Remove them to a separate bowl. The onion will take the longest to soften and burn. Press it with the tongs to see whether it has softened before removing to a chopping board to cool down.

As soon as they are at a temperature you can handle, remove the skins and seeds from the peppers. You can leave any little specks of black as they will add to the smokiness. Don't be tempted to wash them off or you will lose all the flavour. Slit the aubergines open lengthways with a little knife and use a spoon to scoop out all the soft white flesh. You want to get as close to the aubergine skin as possible for the flavour. Then simply peel off and discard the outer layer of the onion, and cut the softened bulb into quarters.

Place all the vegetables on a board and chop roughly so you can still see all the different colours and textures. Transfer to a large mixing bowl and add the lemon juice, vinegar, garlic, parsley, mint, sea salt and oil. Mix well and taste. You may need a touch more salt, but you want to be able to taste every single vegetable.

We like to serve this with some yogurt – sheep's or goats' yogurt works best – and *zehug*, our green coriander relish (page 16).

Poached quince with curd cheese & honeyed hazelnuts

Unlike many European cheeses, most Middle Eastern cheeses are fresh, white and have a strong milky taste which we love. I like to make my own curd – almost a lost tradition these days – but you can also do as my lazy husband would and buy supermarket ricotta. I like my curd soft so I make it on the day of serving, but if you prefer a firmer cheese, start it the night before, add another teaspoon of salt to the mix and leave it hanging overnight. If you can't source quince, try this recipe with pears instead, but note that they will take half the time to cook. Pears don't have that special quince texture, but are a good substitute nonetheless. Even if you aren't going to make your own curd – or indeed make this recipe – do try making the honeyed hazelnuts. They are one of the tastiest preparations in this book and need no accompaniment. You can use as much sea salt and chilli as you dare; they'll be the better for it.

Serves 4 as a starter or 2 as a light main

1 large bag of lamb's lettuce or baby spinach (about 100g), washed
1 small bunch of mint (about 15–20g), picked

For the quince
2 large quinces (or 3 pears)
juice of 1 lemon
100g caster sugar
1 cinnamon stick

For the curd cheese (this makes about 250g curd cheese – enough for this recipe)
550ml full fat milk (you can use goats' milk if you prefer)
100ml single cream
150g natural yogurt
1 tsp salt
juice of 1–2 lemons

For the honeyed hazelnuts
100g roasted whole hazelnuts
1 heaped tbsp honey
a pinch of chilli flakes
a generous pinch of sea salt

For the vinaigrette
1 tbsp olive oil
1 tsp cider vinegar
1 tsp honey
salt and pepper, to taste

Start by cutting each quince (unpeeled) into eight segments and removing the cores with a sharp knife (if you are using pears, quarter them instead). Place in a pan, cover with water and add the lemon juice, sugar and cinnamon stick. Bring to a boil and simmer until the fruit is soft (about 10–15 minutes), then remove from the heat and leave to cool in its poaching liquor in the pan.

Pour the milk and the cream for the curd into a different pan and bring to the boil over a high heat, stirring to avoid burning. Watch it – you don't turn your back on a pot of boiling milk. As soon as it has boiled, add the yogurt and salt and mix through. Return to the boil, then drizzle the juice of one of the lemons all over the milk. You will see it start to split. Leave it on the heat and don't stir, so as not to interfere with the curd formation. Allow to boil for 2 minutes, then turn the heat off. You should see that the curd has separated from the whey; if it hasn't, you may be missing some acidity so add the juice from the second lemon and boil for another couple of minutes until the mixture splits.

Allow to sit for 5 minutes. You can then either use a cheesecloth in a large bowl for the next step, or do as I do and use an unworn stocking inside a tall, narrow vase, folding the top over the sides to hold it in place. Carefully pour the curds and whey into the cheesecloth or stocking and leave to rest for another 10 minutes, with the material still sitting in the whey. Then lift it out and hang to drip-dry (I tie the stocking to the tap over the sink to drip there). I like my curd soft so I only leave it hanging for up to 30 minutes, but you can make a firmer cheese by adding another teaspoon of salt to the milk mixture when you are boiling it and then hanging it overnight; the next day it should resemble a feta.

To prepare the hazelnuts, simply break them up a little and mix with the honey, chilli and salt in a small bowl. When you are ready to serve, mix all the vinaigrette ingredients in a bowl or jug, then use to dress the lamb's lettuce (or spinach) and mint leaves.

We like to serve this on individual plates with a little mound of dressed leaves at the top of the plate, then the quince wedges at the bottom left, followed by a spoonful of the curd cheese at the bottom right and the honeyed hazelnuts on top of the curd.

You can sprinkle with more chilli flakes, if you want, and some freshly ground black pepper.

Any leftover quince syrup can be used to make iced tea (page 273) or saved and used to poach the next batch, as the flavour will intensify.

Peaches & goats' cheese with roasted almonds

This is my wife's favourite salad. She is mad for peaches but for the longest time could not touch them – the feel of the fuzzy skin made her gag. As a child her mom would peel them for her; later in life I got that job. She handles them better now. I think that peaches are treated somehow so they are not as fuzzy as they used to be, or maybe 15 years of cooking has rid her of that squeamishness. If you suffer from the same affliction, use nectarines instead, but the flat white peaches (also known as doughnut peaches) that are to be found in mid-summer are amazing for this recipe, and the combination with fresh coriander and roasted almonds is just perfect.

A light starter for 3–4

1 round lettuce (the soft-leaved one),
  broken into leaves and washed
3 flat white peaches, each cut into 8 segments
120g soft rindless goats' cheese
50g roasted almonds, roughly chopped
4–5 sprigs of coriander, picked
a touch of sea salt
a pinch of freshly ground black pepper

For the dressing
  2 tbsp olive oil
  1 tbsp white wine vinegar
  ½ tsp orange blossom water
  ½ tsp Demerara sugar
  a pinch of salt

Arrange the soft leaves as a base on a serving plate, then top with the peaches, goats' cheese, almonds and coriander leaves. Sprinkle with a touch of sea salt and grind a little black pepper over the top.

Shake the dressing ingredients around in a small jar or airtight container, then spoon over the entire salad. Serve and watch it disappear.

Light Dinners.

We hired Chelsea to be our evening waitress – a 19-year-old the size of a toddler, brimming with energy and cheer. She lived in a big house in Palmers Green with her brother; five sisters; their various partners and friends; a dog; a parrot; and her mum, Adele, a gifted chef and a free spirit who had had a few restaurants in South Africa before she moved her brood to north London.

These kids grew up in Adele's restaurants – serving, cleaning, chopping, chatting – so Chelsea had no trouble fitting in at Honey & Co, taking the job in her stride. She and Rachael fell instantly in love, and Rachael took her on as the little sister she never had. For the first few weeks they were inseparable. They would approach tables together, Rachael always introducing them in her northern accent: 'I'm Rachael, this is Chelsea.' They would go out after work to a spot down the road that they called 'the vibrating pizza place' and stay up all night drinking cheap wine in Fitzroy Square.

At the time we were only open for lunches. We were pleased with our lunch offering but we wanted dinner to be something different, and we were not sure what. We were bouncing ideas off each other, tactfully ignoring Chelsea's teenage notions ('Let's do Mexican nights! With hats and maracas!') and trying different menus. Eventually we decided to do a set menu. As it was a particularly wet August our theme would be 'Somewhere in the world it's summer', and we had a terrific menu full of summery things – corn on the cob, watermelon, grilled prawns... The girls spread the word and our ten tables quickly got booked.

Sarit and I were downstairs cooking. Chelsea and Rachael were setting up the restaurant. We gave them a packet of tea-lights, forgetting to tell them not to use all of them, which of course they did, making the place look like the set of a cheap horror flick or a Gothic funeral.

On the drab, cold August evening our guests started to arrive, and it all started to go wrong. The couples on tables 9 and 10 were both regulars whom we like a lot; they are neighbours, it turns out, who share a stairway and argue every morning about prams in the hallway, and every evening about booming music. The party of four on table 4 were residents of Fitzroy Square who grew frosty when they recognised Rachael and Chelsea as the girls who came to get drunk in the square at night. At first they wanted to leave, but then they decided to stay and make the girls as uncomfortable as they could. And although the room was quite warm from a hundred tea-lights burning, the rain on the window meant that no one was in the mood for ice lollies and watermelons. The night came to its end slowly, horribly, and to cap it all poor Rachael, always so graceful, slipped on a piece of chicken that someone had dropped and glided across the entire restaurant on her bum. She ran downstairs and would not go back up until everyone had left, so embarrassed was she. (I have my suspicions that the harpies on table 4 tripped her.)

By the end of it we were all battered and bruised (Rachael more than the rest of us) and none of us wanted to open for dinner again. Indeed it took us another six months before we opened for dinner full-time, and perhaps longer before we were completely satisfied with what we had to offer. I'd like to say that that night was the worst and it was all plain sailing from then on, but unfortunately that has not always been the case; we've had many a bump along the road to our perfect dinner. We now offer an à la carte menu for starter-main-dessert-type meals, and a set menu with an epic mezze selection, which is more what we are about.

The recipes in this chapter are for light, bright-flavoured main courses, and although some of them require a bit of attention, most are as simple to make as they are to eat.

Lamb siniya

Make this instead of a shepherd's pie the next time you buy lamb mince for dinner. It is just as easy, and though the flavours are distinctly Middle Eastern, this dish pushes the same buttons of comfort and domestic joy. A tomato salad on the side will cut through the richness nicely, and a bit of flat bread will help to mop everything up.

Dinner for 4–6 (there is not much meat but the topping is quite rich)

1 small cauliflower, broken into florets
   (about 350g)
1 litre water
1 tsp salt

For the lamb
   2 onions, peeled and finely chopped
      (about 200g)
   2 tbsp vegetable oil
   ½ tsp + ½ tsp salt
   500g minced lamb
   1 tsp coarsely ground fennel seeds
   2 tbsp baharat spice mix (page 12)
   1 tbsp tomato purée

For the topping
   200g natural yogurt
   200g tahini paste
   2 eggs
   1 tbsp lemon juice
   ½ tsp salt
   1–2 tbsp water (if needed)
   2 tbsp pine nuts

1 tbsp chopped parsley, to serve

Place the cauliflower in a saucepan with the water and salt. Bring to the boil and cook for 5–6 minutes until the florets are soft. Drain and place in a shallow saucepan or casserole dish (about 22cm in diameter).

Fry the onions on a medium heat in a frying pan with the oil and half a teaspoon of salt until the onions start to go golden. Add the minced lamb and the other half-teaspoon of salt, increase the heat to high and use a spoon to break the meat into little pieces. When the lamb starts to brown, sprinkle on the ground fennel and *baharat* spice and cook for 3–4 minutes. Stir in the tomato purée and continue to stir while cooking for a further 3 minutes, then spread all over the cauliflower in the casserole dish. You can prepare this stage up to a day in advance – just cool, cover and store in the refrigerator until needed.

Preheat the oven to 180°C/160°C fan/gas mark 4.

Mix all the topping ingredients together apart from the water and pine nuts. If the mixture is very thick, stir in enough of the water to loosen slightly – the consistency should resemble thick yogurt. Spread the topping over the lamb in the dish. Sprinkle the pine nuts all over and bake in the centre of the oven for 15 minutes or until the tahini looks set and slightly golden. Sprinkle with the parsley and serve.

Sea bream with grapes, cucumber & yogurt

Amorgos, Greece. Our mission was to go to every beach on the island. We drove down to a secluded cove. There was a small boat on the sand, some cars, a little hut of a restaurant... of course we walked in. Not quite a restaurant; more someone's home with a lot of tables in the living room. A gnarly old man came up to us and said, 'Fish' – possibly the only English word he knew. We asked, 'Fish?', he answered 'Fish!' and beckoned us to follow him into the kitchen. He opened a fridge and pulled out a tray, proudly proclaiming 'Fish!' again. Not a lot, but what good fish! I pointed at a bonito, Sarit pointed at a beautiful bream. We went to a table. We had beer and he brought us some salad. Half an hour later the bonito came, gently fried, with half a lemon and fried potatoes that tasted of potatoes and sand. Half an hour after that, the bream arrived, same garnish. We ate with our fingers, peeling flakes of sweet salty flesh from the bone. It was embarrassingly cheap. We left a gigantic tip and stayed the rest of the afternoon on that beach, in and out of the water.

Dinner for 4

4 small Lebanese cucumbers or 2 long ones
* (about 600g)*
250g red grapes
4 sprigs of fresh mint, leaves picked
1 small bunch of dill, fronds picked off
* the main stem*
1 tbsp lemon (juice of ½ lemon)
1 tsp sea salt
½ tsp freshly ground black pepper
3 tbsp olive oil, plus 2 tbsp for frying
200g yogurt (goats' is best)
2 large sea bream, scaled and filleted (4 fillets)
½ lemon

Peel a couple of strips along the length of each cucumber to create a zebra-striped effect when you chop. Slice them in half lengthways and use a teaspoon to scoop out the seeds. Chop into thin crescents and place in a large bowl.

Wash and halve the grapes, then add to the cucumbers. Roughly chop the mint and dill, and add them too. Season with the lemon juice, salt, pepper and olive oil and mix well. Spread 2 tablespoons of the yogurt on each of the four plates. Pile the grape and cucumber salad in the centre, ready for the fish.

Heat the remaining 2 tablespoons of olive oil in a heavy-based frying pan. Place the fillets skin-side down in the pan and season with a little sea salt and pepper. Allow 1–2 minutes so that the skin crisps up, then flip the fillets carefully and cook for 2 minutes on the other side. Squeeze the half lemon over the fish while still in the pan and allow to sizzle. Then carefully remove the fillets and place one on top of each of the prepared plates. Serve straight away.

Beef kofta

Another dish that started by the beach, this one in Tel Aviv, in a place simply called 'The Bulgarian', where you'd get a loaf of white bread, white aubergine purée, roasted red peppers, white bean salad simply seasoned with onion and parsley, and very moreish kofta. We kept trying to figure out what went in them – the owner was such a crabby guy we didn't dare to ask. Eventually we came up with these, which are a close approximation. The cheese and the caraway make a terrific combo, seasoning without overpowering, and the texture is great too. Lovely by themselves; lovelier with this salad, which can be made in advance.

**Dinner for 4
(allows 3 kofta
per person)**

For the kofta
2 slices of thick white bread
   (or leftover milk bun, page 67)
enough milk to soak the bread
   (about 240ml)
1 large onion, peeled (about 120g)
3 cloves of garlic, peeled
600g beef mince
4 tsp whole caraway seeds
1 tsp salt
½ tsp ground white pepper
1½ tsp bicarbonate of soda
130g kashkaval cheese, finely grated
   (you can use pecorino instead)

For the bean salad
150g dried cannellini beans, soaked
   overnight in plenty of water
1 small onion, peeled and halved but with
   the stalk kept on
2 sticks of celery
2 cloves of garlic, peeled and crushed
5 sprigs of thyme, picked
2 red Romano peppers
1 aubergine
1 small red onion, peeled and diced as
   small as you can (about 80g)
1 small bunch of parsley, chopped
   (about 15–20g)
1 tbsp red wine vinegar
2 tbsp olive oil

Remove the crusts from the bread and soak it in the cold milk for 10 minutes. In the meantime purée the onion and garlic together in a food processor till completely smooth (or grate them on a fine grater if you prefer). Squeeze the soaked bread and put in a large bowl with all the other kofta ingredients. Mix well until combined.

Divide the mixture into 12 balls of about 80g each (about the size of a clementine). Cover and chill for at least an hour before cooking. This will help the flavours to combine and enable the protein in the meat to stick everything together.

Drain the cannellini beans and place them in a pan with the onion and celery. Cover with fresh water and bring to boil, then skim any foam that has formed and lower the heat to a simmer. Keep on cooking until the beans are soft and most of the water has evaporated – the beans won't be covered in water any more but there should be some liquid left in the pan. Cooking times may vary depending on how fresh the beans are.

Remove the pan from the heat and discard the celery and onion. Add the crushed garlic cloves and thyme leaves to the hot beans and season with salt and pepper. Cover the pot and allow to cool.

In the meantime set your grill to the highest setting. Grill the peppers and aubergine, turning occasionally, until they are charred all over – this will take about 20 minutes. When they are cool enough to handle, peel and shred them into long strips (there's more detailed advice on how to do this on page 85).

Mix the pepper, aubergine, beans, red onion, parsley, red wine vinegar and oil together well and adjust the seasoning to taste. If you're preparing the salad in advance, don't add the parsley or adjust the seasoning until just before you serve.

To cook the kofta, set your grill to the highest setting again. Lightly grease a roasting tin or baking tray and place the kofta on it with a little space around each one. Cook for about 6 minutes, then turn them and cook on the other side for another 6 minutes. They should be a roasted brown colour and be bouncy to the touch.

Lay the kofta on the bean salad and serve. The kofta juices in the roasting tin are a cook's treat to be mopped with bread, but if you are feeling generous, you can pour them on top of the whole thing.

Pomegranate molasses chicken with bulgar wheat salad

This is a good one to make when people come round, as it is really hard not to like – sweet and sour, plenty of textures, pretty colours and virtually everybody likes chicken. Using chicken thighs here makes it almost impossible to dry the meat out and ensures plenty of chicken flavour to come through the strong marinade.

Dinner for 4

8 chicken thigh fillets, skin removed
1 tbsp vegetable oil, for frying

For the marinade
  2 cloves of garlic, peeled and sliced
  ½ –1 green chilli (depends how hot you like it), sliced
  3 tbsp pomegranate molasses
  1 tbsp vegetable oil
  ½ tsp freshly ground black pepper

For the salad
  200g bulgar wheat
  ½ tsp salt
  1 tsp olive oil
  200ml boiling water
  50g shelled pistachios, roasted and coarsely chopped (half reserved to sprinkle on top)
  75g currants
  2 tsp dried mint
  1 tbsp pomegranate molasses
  50g fresh pomegranate seeds (1 tbsp reserved to sprinkle over the top)
  1 small bunch of mint, roughly chopped (about 15–20g)
  1 small bunch of parsley, roughly chopped (about 15–20g)

Mix the marinade ingredients together and use to coat the chicken all over. Cover and keep in the fridge for a minimum of 2 hours to marinate. You can start the meat marinating up to 48 hours in advance – just leave it in the fridge until you are ready to start cooking.

Preheat the oven to 200°C/180°C fan/gas mark 6.

Place the bulgar wheat in a bowl with the salt and oil, pour over the boiling water and cover with cling film for 5 minutes. Uncover and fluff up the bulgar using a fork. Add all the remaining salad ingredients except those you have reserved to use as garnish, and stir well.

Heat the vegetable oil in a large frying pan over a medium heat and place the chicken thighs smooth-side down in it. Season with salt and pepper and fry for 2–3 minutes until the thighs go a lovely dark golden colour, then flip them over and cook for a further 2 minutes. Place the frying pan in the oven for 12 minutes, by which time the chicken should be cooked through.

Spoon the salad onto individual plates or a large serving platter and top with the chicken and the juices that have accumulated in the frying pan. Sprinkle with the reserved pistachios and pomegranate seeds to garnish.

Prawns in orange, tomato & cardamom

I tried this with supermarket pre-peeled raw prawns and it still tasted great, but if you can get your hands on whole large Mediterranean prawns with the heads still attached, you'll not only enjoy their sweet flesh but the heads will ooze their lovely juices into the sauce, making it richer in that particular prawny flavour. If you are using pre-peeled prawns, you will need to add some more water to the pan to create a proper sauce.

This is a great dinner for 2 (or 1 greedy prawn-lover like me...)

2 tbsp olive oil
1 orange, thinly sliced
2 tomatoes, thinly sliced
2 cloves of garlic, peeled and thinly sliced
2 sprigs of fresh thyme
½ small red chilli, seeds removed and
    thinly sliced
3 cardamom pods, crushed to reveal
    the black seeds
12–14 large prawns (about 200g once peeled)
sea salt
freshly ground black pepper
3–5 tbsp water

Heat the oil in a frying pan over a high heat until it just starts to smoke. Carefully place the orange slices in the oil and cook for 30 seconds, then turn them over with a fork. Add the tomato, garlic, thyme, chilli and cardamom and cook on a high heat until the tomato slices start to break down a little (about 2 minutes). Add the prawns to the pan and season with sea salt and pepper. Cook them for a minute on each side. Add 3 tablespoons of water and cook for a further 2 minutes or until the prawns have turned pink. If the pan is looking dry, add the remaining 2 tablespoons of water, so that you have enough liquid to form a sauce.

Serve immediately with bread to mop up the juices. Alternatively munch all the prawns by yourself in the kitchen, mop the pan with bread and use it to prepare an omelette for your dining partner. Make sure you don't have sauce on your lips when you leave the kitchen and say the prawns are ruined and that you're not hungry.

Lamb salad with Georgian plum sauce

There are so many terrific preparations using unripe fruit, which adds a different and exciting shade of sourness – stews studded with sour grapes, crunchy melon pickles, green tomato salads. These are really hard to come by unless you grow your own, as all the fruit in the supermarkets tends to be either super-sweet or bland. That said, we do manage to find sour plums at Tesco, at least at the one in Brixton, where the supermarket management saw fit to plant a few plum trees in the vast parking lot. You can pick as many as you want, no one will say anything, and you don't need to pay for them – that's Tesco value for you. This is our version of *tkemali*, a sauce made with sour plums (made with sweet ones and vinegar here) that is the Georgian equivalent of ketchup. It works with most meats and grilled oily fish, but is particularly good with lamb.

A light dinner for 2

For the lamb
1 tbsp vegetable oil
½ tsp freshly ground fennel seeds
½ tsp ground cumin
400g lamb leg steak or rump
a generous sprinkling of sea salt and
    freshly ground black pepper

For the plum sauce
2–3 large red plums, de-stoned and roughly
    sliced (about 150g)
½ tsp whole fennel seeds
1 clove of garlic, peeled and cut in
    half lengthways
2 tbsp Demerara sugar
4 tbsp white wine vinegar
a little water (if needed)
½ tsp sea salt (if needed)

For the salad
1 large bag of lamb's lettuce or baby
    spinach (about 100g)
2 plums, cut into thin wedges
1 small bunch of tarragon (about 15–20g),
    picked

Set a heavy-bottomed frying pan on the stove on a medium-to-low heat. Mix the oil with the spices in a small bowl and rub over the lamb. Sprinkle with the salt and pepper, then place the meat in the pan and sear all over – you will need to give it about 2 minutes after every turn; the whole process should take about 10–12 minutes. Keep the heat on a steady medium-to-low so that the meat has a chance to start cooking but you also get a deep brown crust. Remove the lamb from the pan, leaving the pan on the stove to use for the sauce (it is important to use the same pan as it has all the lovely lamby flavours in it). Cover the meat with some aluminium foil and allow to rest while you prepare the sauce.

Increase the heat under the pan to high and add the sliced plums, fennel seeds and garlic. Stir for 1 minute, then add the sugar and mix well. Pour in the vinegar, reduce the heat to medium and allow the plums to soften. They should take about 10 minutes to cook, depending on how soft they are to start with. You may need to add a little water while cooking to loosen the sauce – the end result should be like a very runny jam. Taste and see whether it needs the salt.

Place the salad leaves on a serving plate and scatter on the plum wedges and tarragon. Cut the lamb into thin slices and arrange on top. Spoon the warm sauce all over and serve.

Mint and lemon chicken with apricots & potatoes

There are two weeks out of 52 in which apricots are available, good and cheap, and during that fortnight we add them to everything. This dish is a particularly good match with apricots, but in the other 50 weeks, make it without them – the potatoes cooked under the chicken, absorbing all the goodness, are just as good all year round.

An easy dinner for a hungry 4 or a shy 5

1 kg chicken thighs (or, if you prefer, a whole chicken cut in pieces)
2–3 large potatoes, peeled and cut in long thin wedges
2 red onions, peeled and cut into 8 wedges each
1 head of garlic, broken into cloves but not peeled
1 lemon, cut in wedges
8–10 apricots, halved
2 tsp sea salt

For the marinade
  2 tbsp dried mint
  1 tsp sumac
  1 tsp chilli flakes
  1 tsp freshly ground black pepper
  2 tbsp olive oil

For the mint salsa
  2 preserved lemons (page 14), chopped
  1 small bunch of mint (about 15–20g), picked and roughly chopped
  2 tbsp olive oil
  1 tsp sumac

Mix all the marinade ingredients together with the chicken pieces to coat thoroughly, then cover and set in the fridge to marinate for at least 1 hour (it can wait for a few hours, if you can).

Preheat the oven to 220°C/200°C fan/gas mark 7.

Put the prepared vegetables and fruit in a large roasting tray and place the chicken pieces on top. Sprinkle the sea salt all over. Roast in the top of the oven for 20 minutes, then mix everything around a little, making sure the fruit and vegetables get coated in the fat at the bottom of the tray. Return to the oven for a further 10–15 minutes until everything is golden and crisp.

While the chicken is cooking, mix the salsa ingredients together in a small bowl. Spoon over the hot chicken pieces before serving.

Red mullet with artichoke & preserved lemons

These pretty fish are the prize of the Med with their sweet flesh and tight flakes – they are unlike any other. Dipped in flour, fried and served simply with fresh lemon, they make for a meal that is hard to beat, but this artichoke and preserved lemon treatment really highlights their unique flavour. This dish also works extremely well with bream, another Mediterranean star. We allow 150–200g filleted fish per person, but you can double the amount of fish without having to double the rest; there is plenty of good sauce to go round.

Dinner for 2

1 large or 2 small red mullet, descaled, gutted and filleted (about 300–400g)
6 baby artichokes (or 2 large globe artichoke hearts)
vegetable oil, for shallow frying
1 red onion, peeled (about 100g)
2 cloves of garlic, peeled
2 preserved lemons (page 14)
2 tbsp olive oil
2 tbsp ras el hanut spice mix
1 cinnamon stick
480ml water
30g plain flour
½ tsp salt
a generous pinch of freshly ground black pepper
a handful of chopped coriander, to garnish

Cut the fillets into chunky pieces – enough for about 2–3 bites from each piece. If I have a large mullet, I usually cut it in half lengthways, remove the dark red blood line and cut each strip into three, but if you have two small mullets, just cutting each fillet in half or thirds will be fine. Set the fish pieces on some kitchen paper in the fridge to wait while you prepare the next stages.

Clean the artichokes to reveal the hearts (see method on page 46) and cut them into quarters (or wedges, if using large ones). Place a frying pan on the stove, fill with about 2cm of vegetable oil and set the heat on medium-high. Fry the artichoke segments in the oil, turning them occasionally, until they start going a lovely golden colour. This will not take very long – about 3–4 minutes. Remove and place on a plate lined with some kitchen paper to drain any excess oil. Reserve the oil in the frying pan for cooking the fish.

Purée the onion and garlic to a pulp; you can grate them if you don't have a food processor. Halve the preserved lemons and discard any seeds. Cut one half into thin strips and place these on the kitchen paper with the fried artichokes. Purée the remaining lemon halves.

Place the olive oil and puréed onion-garlic mixture in a deep frying pan and cook on a medium high heat, stirring occasionally, until the juices evaporate and it dries out. Add the ras el hanut and cinnamon stick and stir to coat. Tip in the preserved lemon purée, stir well to combine and allow to cook for 1 minute. Stir in the water, bring to the boil, then reduce the heat and simmer for 10 minutes.

While the sauce is simmering, combine the flour, salt and pepper in a flat dish. Reheat the oil-filled frying pan over a medium-high heat. You can test that it is hot enough by dropping in a pinch of flour – it should fizz up. Dip each piece of fish in the seasoned flour to coat, then place carefully in the oil, skin-side down (don't overcrowd the pan; you can fry the fish in two batches if need be). Fry the skin-side for 2 minutes, then flip the pieces over to fry the other side for 30 seconds. Remove to the plate with the lemon strips and fried artichokes to drain.

Once the sauce has had 10 minutes simmering, carefully place the artichokes, lemon pieces and fried fish in the sauce and leave to cook for 4 minutes. Serve with some couscous and sprinkle with the chopped coriander.

3 Ashtanur griddle bread recipes

My good friend Ben has been happily married to my good friend Inbal, an Israeli girl, for over ten years now, but I think he still dies a bit every time they walk into a café and his wife sends her coffee back or asks if there are any sandwiches with 'normal' fillings, by which she means 'normal in Israel'. He is a terrific cook, fascinated by Asian cuisine. He will construct delicately balanced curries and stir-fries, only to hear his wife ask 'Can we not have regular food tonight?', by which she means 'regular in Israel'. And he, like a true English gent, will say, 'Sure darling. I'll put it in a pitta for you.' In these recipes the flatbread serves as a plate: you place your charred meat in the middle with sauce and salad. You can use cutlery or go native and tear bits of bread from the edges with your fingers to use to grab bits of meat. You'll end up with the bit of bread in the middle that has soaked up all the juices; it's the best bit, like an artichoke's heart.

BBQ beef with tomato salad on griddle bread

Dinner for 2

350–400 g sirloin steak (a personal favourite; you can use other cuts if you prefer)
2 ashtanur griddle breads (page 62)
2 tbsp olive oil for searing the steak

For the onion marinade
3 cloves of garlic, peeled
1 small onion, peeled (about 100g)
1 tsp salt
1 tsp smoky paprika
1 tsp ground cumin
½ tsp ground pimento (allspice)
½ tsp cayenne pepper

For the tomato and chilli salad
1 punnet of the best cherry tomatoes you can find (about 200g)
½ small green chilli, deseeded and diced
1 small bunch of coriander, chopped (about 15–20g)
2 tbsp olive oil
1 tbsp red wine vinegar
salt and pepper, to taste

For the paprika yogurt dressing
100g natural yogurt
1 tbsp olive oil
a pinch of salt and pepper
1 tsp smoky paprika

Purée the marinade ingredients together in a food processor to make a paste, then rub it all over the steaks. Cover and place in the fridge. Allow the meat to rest in the marinade for a minimum of 1 hour and up to 48 hours, but beware – the meat will soften more and more, so no longer or it will become mushy.

Halve the cherry tomatoes and mix with all the other salad ingredients. Mix all the yogurt dressing ingredients together in a small jug or glass.

Now you are just left with the hugely satisfying job of searing your steak. Set a heavy skillet or griddle on the stove and allow it to heat fully before adding the oil. Lift the meat out of the marinade and place in the pan. Sear on one side for 2 minutes without touching it, then carefully lift and flip to the other side. Allow another 2–3 minutes; you can let it cook for a little longer if you want, but I think this is just perfect. Remove from the pan to a plate, cover lightly with some aluminium foil and allow to rest for 5–10 minutes.

Halve the salad between the two griddle breads, drizzle with the yogurt dressing and then cut thick, lush slices of meat to place on top.

Pan-fried chicken liver with grapes on griddle bread

Don't be liver-phobic, as this is one of the tastiest dishes in this book, and even in the fanciest butcher's the finest livers are very cheap to buy. We use a Turkish grape molasses called *pekmez* in this recipe. If you can't find it, I have provided a recipe to make your own grape sauce.

4 ashtanur griddle breads (page 62)

Dinner for 4

For the onions
2 large onions, peeled
½ tsp salt
1 tbsp olive oil
1 tbsp white wine vinegar
2 bay leaves

For the livers
800g fresh chicken livers
1 tsp salt
½ tsp freshly ground black pepper
¼ – ½ tsp chilli flakes
   (depending on your preference)
½ tsp ground cumin
2 tbsp olive oil
a knob of butter (about 25g)
½ bunch of fresh black grapes,
   washed and halved (about 160g)
1 cinnamon stick
160g pekmez grape syrup or home-made
   grape sauce (see below)
1 tsp sumac
a handful of parsley leaves, picked whole

For the home-made grape sauce
200g black grapes, washed and halved
2 tbsp sugar
1 tbsp balsamic or Corinthian wine vinegar

Preheat the oven to 200°C/180°C fan/ gas mark 6.

Slice the onions into rings about as thick as your little finger. Set them on a small roasting tray, add the salt, olive oil, vinegar and bay leaves and toss around to coat. Cover the tray with aluminium foil and place in the oven to soften but not colour. Check after 15 minutes and mix everything around – the onions should be soft. Turn the heat off, re-cover the tray with foil and return to the oven to keep warm until you are ready to eat.

If you don't have any *pekmez*, you will need to make the grape sauce. It is actually very easy. Heat a frying pan on a high heat. Toss in the grapes and sugar, allow the juices to start running out, then add the vinegar and reduce to a syrup. This will only take about 5 minutes. Use a potato masher to squish the juice out of the grapes, then remove the pan from the heat. You can strain the sauce if you want, but I think the texture is rather nice.

Remove any white membrane or dis-coloured bits from the livers and separate each one into two lobes (or ask your butcher to prepare the livers for you). Season with the salt, pepper, chilli flakes and cumin. Heat the oil and butter together in a large frying pan on a medium-high heat and fry the liver in two or three batches, as you don't want to crowd the pan. Be careful, as the liver will spit. Allow about 1 minute on each side until the pieces are nicely browned, then remove to a bowl and fry the next batch. Once they are all seared, return the livers and any accumulated juices to the pan and add the fresh grapes, cinnamon stick and *pekmez* or grape sauce. Sauté for 3–4 minutes on a high heat until the livers go all glossy.

Place a griddle bread on each plate and spoon on the warm onions. Top with the glossy liver, sprinkle with the sumac and parsley leaves, serve as soon as you can and ask yourself how come you don't eat liver more often.

Roasted sea bream with spring onions on griddle bread

2 ashtanur *griddle breads (page 62)*

Dinner for 2

1 large bream, gutted and de-scaled
(about 500g)
1 lemon
6 spring onions
2 cloves of garlic
½ tsp ground fennel
½ tsp ground coriander
½ tsp ground cardamom pods (page 11)
½ tsp sea salt
1 head of Little Gem lettuce

For the mayonnaise
1 egg yolk
120ml olive oil
a pinch of salt

Start by roasting the bream. Heat your oven to 220°C/200°C fan/gas mark 7. Take a large sheet of greaseproof paper (big enough to wrap the fish in) and set it on a large sheet of aluminium foil (slightly larger than the greaseproof sheet). Slice one half of the lemon into at least four slices and place three of them in the centre of the paper.

Chop the green part of the spring onions and reserve for later. Place the white bulbs with the lemon slices. Halve and peel the garlic cloves, and place them with the lemon slices too. Slit the fish skin in three places with a sharp knife to reveal some flesh. Mix the spices and salt together, then rub them all over the fish, including inside the stomach. Place another slice of lemon in the stomach and lay the fish on top of the lemon slices, spring onion bulbs and garlic. If there are any remaining lemon slices, place them on top of the fish.

Now lift the sides of the paper and aluminium foil around the fish. Leave some space above the fish, then twist

the edges of the foil to seal the parcel so that there are no air holes. It should look like a long, covered sailboat. Place it in a roasting tray in the oven for 25–30 minutes. After this time check it by carefully opening the bag and moving the flesh a little with a fork – it should come away from the bone easily. Close the package again, remove from the oven and allow to cool.

While you are waiting, shred the lettuce and mix it with the chopped spring onion and the juice of the remaining half lemon. You can add a pinch of salt if you want.

Once the fish is at a temperature you can handle, open the parcel and use a knife to slit the fish down the middle to the bone. Remove the flesh to a side plate. Flip the fish over and repeat on the other side. Discard the skin, bones and lemon slices but lift out all the spring onion bulbs and add to the flesh.

Carefully lift the paper and transfer all the lovely juices (there should be about 2–3 tablespoons) and the garlic cloves to a small mixing bowl. Use the back of a spoon to squash the garlic to a paste. Add the egg yolk and whisk a little, then add the oil at a slow drizzle, whisking all the time to make a special kind of mayonnaise.

Warm the griddle bread and place half the fish and spring onion bulbs in the centre of each one. Top with some lettuce salad and spoon on some mayonnaise before serving. Serve the remaining mayo on the side so you can top up as you go. Or boil some baby potatoes to dip in it.

Balls &
Stuff.

One of our favourite restaurants in the world is called Restaurant Margaret and Victor (RIP) Tayar. It is little more than a hut on the beach in Jaffa, an ugly concrete balcony facing the most beautiful sea scene. The humble plastic tables and chairs are dressed in tablecloths that look like, and indeed are, old bed sheets. The brilliance of the food comes as an utter surprise, as does the magnitude of the bill.

The food you eat there is the stuff of dreams – charred peppers with preserved lemon and mint sauce, sweet and spicy beets with currants, white aubergine purée, red aubergine purée, fried marinated aubergines, vine leaves, gorgeous hummus... and these are just the starters. The couscous dishes are second to none. The grouper kofta are legendary. There are sardines stuffed with coriander and cod's roe, and beef and potato *mafrum*, everything bright and electric with flavour.

Margaret learned to cook from the husband she outlived (as the restaurant name suggests), and makes the old, traditional North African dishes with a talent and care that are all her own. The little restaurant is filled to the brim with her Gypsy good looks and laughter. She leaves the kitchen after service to do everyone's bill – a mysterious procedure that only she can perform – and takes into account many more things than simply the food that was ordered. You can hear her saying to a regular customer, 'If I'd known it was you, I would have given you the good fish,' or see her smiling at an outraged couple whose lunch has cost the same as a car. The price of magic.

Every morning the fishermen bring her the night's catch, and she goes through it meticulously, suspicious of the freshness and provenance of every specimen, trusting no one and nothing but her senses. A few times during the winter a truck full of tiny, sweet lemons unloads at the restaurant. These are rumoured to come from a grove in the Sinai desert in Egypt and will be preserved for use in next year's cooking. Twice a week she goes to market to choose the fruit, herbs and vegetables she will cook in the restaurant, and she arranges the boxes on her balcony in colourful rows – lemons, squashes, peppers, aubergines. If you ask her what the secret of her food is, she says it's all about leaving the fruit and vegetables outdoors: the sun concentrates their flavour and gives them sweetness, while the sea breeze gives them a bit of salt. I'm not sure how scientific this theory is. I always thought that perhaps she left it all outside because she had no room inside, or that she was just being lazy, but I respect the humility of such a great cook before her ingredients.

The recipes in this chapter are perhaps the heart of our restaurant, and the heart of this book. They range from the slightly fussy to the painfully time-consuming. These are the kinds of things that are prepared by mothers and grandmothers who spend their days at kitchen tables, with ample time for rolling, wrapping, scraping and stuffing – procedures so arduous that you cannot mistake the resulting dishes for anything but the labour of much care. At Honey & Co our only goal is to make tasty food, but if we were to have any other mission statement or ideology, it would be to serve and preserve these recipes which nobody else has time for any more... although we try not to have more than a couple of these labour-intensive dishes on the menu at any one time.

Beetroot kubbe soup

Kubbe dumpling soup is the jewel in the crown of many kitchens all along the Fertile Crescent; there are endless variations on the dough, the filling and the soup. This version is easy in comparison to some others we came across, but is extremely satisfying in taste and looks, and as comforting as only home food can be.

Makes about 12 dumplings, which should be enough for 4 people

For the dumpling dough
250g semolina
200ml water
1½ tsp salt

For the filling
1 onion, grated or minced (about 80g)
½ tsp salt
150g minced beef
a pinch of white pepper
1 tbsp baharat *spice mix (page 12)*

For the soup
1 onion, peeled and roughly chopped
    (about 120g)
1 tbsp olive oil
1 tbsp tomato purée
2 sticks of celery, sliced
1 tomato, grated
2 beetroots, peeled and diced (about 200g)
4 sprigs of parsley, roughly chopped
1 tsp salt
juice of 2 lemons

Mix all the dough ingredients together and set them aside for an hour. At first it will look like a very loose porridge, but after an hour's rest it'll come together (against reason) to a soft, smooth, shiny dough.

While your dough is resting, prepare the soup: start by sautéing the chopped onion in the oil until it starts to soften (about 5 minutes), then add the tomato purée and mix well so that the onion is thoroughly coated.

Add all the other soup ingredients and stir to combine. Cover with 2 litres of water and bring to the boil. Skim any foam that comes to the top and reduce the heat to a simmer. Partially cover the pot and cook for about 30–40 minutes until the beets are soft. The soup should taste quite tangy and have a good amount of salt, as this will be absorbed into the dumplings, so if you think it is a bit bland, add some more. The soup is now ready for the *kubbe* – it will look a bit watery at this stage but that's good, as the semolina in the dough will thicken it considerably.

While the soup is simmering, mix all the filling ingredients together and form into twelve little balls, each about the size of a cherry tomato. If your dough is ready you can make the *kubbe* now, otherwise leave the filling balls in the fridge until it is.

To assemble the *kubbe*, roughly divide the semolina dough into twelve pieces. Dampen your palms with some water and grab a piece of dough – it will seem soft but that is normal. Flatten it on your palm – it should be big enough to cover your palm and about 1cm thick. Place a ball of filling in the centre and fold the edges of the dough over it, sealing the pastry, then pop it into the simmering soup. Repeat with the rest of the dough and filling balls until all twelve dumplings are floating in the soup.

Cook the soup and dumplings for about another 30 minutes on a constant simmer with the lid partially covering the pot. The soup will thicken and the dumplings will plump up. We allow three *kubbe* per person and like to serve this soup in large flat bowls, with some fresh lemon wedges to squeeze over.

The soup and dumplings will keep well in the fridge for a couple of days, but make sure to warm thoroughly before serving.

Whole stuffed chicken with freekeh, almonds & pine nuts

We received our dear friend Shahar (aka 'Couscousul'), along with this nickname, in a package deal from our old employer and good friend Yotam. A skinny man with a big heart and a bigger stomach, Shahar took us under his wing and now guides us through the London jungle. He tells us what films and plays to see, what to read (and what to think about it), where to eat and what's worth doing. He is something of a cult figure at Honey & Co, and everyone becomes giddy with excitement each time he comes to see us, like a godfather or favourite uncle. He has all the time in the world to listen to our gripes, and lets us be a part of his Woody-Allen-ish everyday. To show our gratitude we cook hearty, homey, stick-to-the-ribs-type food for him, just to hear him say – as he does every time – 'This is exactly the kind of food that I like.'

Serves 2–4, depending on whether you eat a thigh and a breast, or can make do with just one of them. Better still, avoid the problem altogether and cook four little chickens (poussins), so you have 1 per person.

135g freekeh (or if you can't get hold of it, use coarse grind bulgar wheat)
1 tsp salt, plus more to season
50g whole almonds, skin on and roughly chopped
50g pine nuts
2 tbsp olive oil
1 small onion, peeled and diced (about 100g)
2 cloves of garlic, peeled and halved
1 orange, sliced thinly with the skin on
2 tsp + 1 tsp sweet spice mix (page 12)
1 knob of fresh ginger, peeled and grated (about 1 tbsp)
1 chicken (about 1–1½ kg) or 4 poussins
1 knob of butter (about 25g)

Wash the freekeh well, drain it and place in a pan. Cover with lots of fresh, cold water and add the teaspoon of salt. Bring to the boil and cook for about 20 minutes, then drain.

Place the almonds and pine nuts in a frying pan over a medium heat and mix while they toast a little – for about 1 minute – before adding the oil, onion and garlic. Sauté until the onion and garlic have softened, then stir in half the orange slices, 2 teaspoons of sweet spice mix and the grated ginger. Cook for another

2 minutes, then tip in the *freekeh* and mix well. Remove from the stove.

If you are cooking one large chicken, preheat your oven to 240°C/220°C fan/gas mark 9.

Now fill the chicken as tightly as you can with as much of the stuffing as you can. If you have a little left over, spoon it into the centre of a roasting dish, place 3 of the uncooked slices of orange on top and lay the chicken on them (if there is no filling left over, just lay the stuffed bird on the three slices of orange in the roasting dish). Try to spread the legs out so that the meat cooks evenly.

Rub the breast and legs of the chicken with the butter and sprinkle the remaining teaspoon of sweet spice all over. Season generously with salt and freshly ground pepper. If you have any uncooked orange slices left over, push them under the skin. This is much easier than it sounds – you just need to grab the flap of skin above the breast and lift it a little, then push the slices between the flesh and the skin.

Make sure the oven is hot before you put the chicken in as this will help to give it a lovely crispy skin. Place the chicken in the centre of the oven and roast for 15 minutes, then reduce the temperature to 200°C/180°C fan/gas mark 6 and cook for a further 15 minutes. Remove from the oven and check that the meat is cooked by inserting a small knife into the thickest part of the thigh – the liquids that come out should be clear. If you think the chicken needs a little more time, cover the breast with a piece of aluminium foil and return it to the oven for 5–6 minutes, but make sure not to dry it out.

If you are using four little poussins instead of one large chicken, preheat your oven to 200°C/180°C fan/gas mark 6 and then stuff, grease and season the birds as above, pushing any remaining orange slices under the skins. The poussins will only need 20 minutes roasting in total, so after 10 minutes at 200°C/180°C fan/gas mark 6, reduce the heat to 180°C/160°C fan/gas mark 4 and roast for another 10 minutes before checking that the meat is cooked through.

You will need a spoon to scoop out all the lovely stuffing. It's nice to carve this dish at the table, and then pick the bones clean with your fingers.

Gundi

In a side street in the red light district of Tel Aviv is an easy-to-miss door sign, simply saying 'Eden'. Though the name may suggest it, it is not a massage parlour or a peep show like the shops next to it; it is a place dedicated to other carnal pleasures. You would walk through a foul-smelling, underlit corridor into a very square room with aluminium chairs, laminate tabletops, ceiling fans, sweaty people, neon, no windows – as far from Eden as you could possibly be. The room is filled with a particular smell: floral, funky, citrusy, deeply savoury. As you sit down, the old girl serving will place some bread and pickles on your table, tahini pungent with fenugreek, and *sabzi* – a platter laden with a mountain of fresh, fragrant herbs and radishes as big as your fist. Every Persian meal is served with this, and the plate will be refilled as it empties. The herbs are used as palate cleanser, as seasoning and as salad. The menu offers all the classic Persian stews and grills, all delicious, but if you're smart you will order *gundi*. What you'll get is a bowl of murky, yellow-ish broth with some chickpeas and a dumpling the size of an orange in the middle. When you taste the dumpling, you'll find it cloudlike and warm with spice; the chicken broth will taste of dried Persian limes and the fresh herbs you added to it from the diminishing mound on your table. Welcome to Eden.

Makes 16 dumplings, which should be enough for 4–6 people

For the soup
- 8–10 chicken wings (about 600g)
- 3 dried Persian limes, cut in half
- 4 celery stalks, whole
- 2 carrots, peeled and cut in half lengthways
- 1 onion, peeled and halved
- 1 tsp whole peppercorns
- 1 tsp whole fennel seeds
- 1 tsp whole coriander seeds
- 1 tsp ground turmeric
- 2 tsp salt
- 3 litres water

For the dumplings
- 500g minced chicken thighs
- 3 onions, peeled and puréed in a food processor or grated (about 300g)
- 100g gram (chickpea) flour
- 60ml vegetable oil
- 1 tsp ground cardamom pods (page 11)
- 1 tsp ground cumin
- 1 tsp turmeric
- 1 tsp salt
- ½ tsp white pepper

soft herbs, leaves and edible flowers (to serve)

Place all the soup ingredients in a very large saucepan and bring to the boil. Skim and reduce the heat to a constant simmer. Partially cover the pot and cook for 1 hour, then turn off the heat and leave for an hour to allow all the flavours to come together. Strain the soup – retain the liquid, discard the vegetables, and the wings can go to a cat you like. Return the liquid to a large pan.

Mix the dumpling ingredients together to form a very soft, wet and squidgy dough. Use wet hands to divide it and form into rough ball shapes of 60g each. Chill for at least an hour in the fridge.

Bring the broth back to the boil, then with damp hands re-form the dumplings into balls and carefully drop them in, making sure they are fully submerged. Return to the boil, then lower the heat, cover the pot and let it simmer for about 50 minutes, during which time the balls will expand and go really fluffy.

We serve three per person with some of the soup and lots of picked soft herbs; dill, chervil, celery leaves, coriander, mint and edible flowers; you can use any or all, and finely sliced radishes for authentic freshness and crunch.

Stuffed vine leaves

The most tortuous of all foods to prepare, this is truly a case of the result justifying the effort. Once you have tasted stuffed vine leaves from the cooking pot, you will understand why tinned ones can never compare. If you are lucky enough to own a vine, then use the fresh leaves – they are amazing when they are young and soft; all you need to do is blanch them for 30 seconds in salt water. But as most of us don't have access to a vine, we buy pre-salted leaves in a jar. Some recipes leave room for personal taste and improvisation, but this is not one of them, at least not until you have made it a few times. The quantities are exact and although it seems like a lot of olive oil, lemon and mint, they are the cornerstones of this dish. It would not be worth making without or with less, so if you are not a fan of lemon or mint, this recipe is not for you.

200g vine leaves (from a jar or
vacuum-packed)

Makes about 30

For the filling
1 tbsp olive oil
½ cinnamon stick
2 white onions, peeled and finely diced
(about 250g)
1 tsp turmeric
a pinch of cayenne
3 tbsp dried mint
250g risotto rice
2 tsp sea salt (or 1 tsp table salt)
juice of 2 lemons (about 120ml)
240ml water
2 small bunches of fresh mint, chopped
(about 30–40g)

To cook
2 leeks (about 300g)
200g green grapes
1 lemon
juice of 2 lemons
120ml olive oil
240ml water

First prepare the leaves – bring a large pot of water to the boil and place the leaves in it. Return to the boil and then remove from the heat. Allow them to sit in the water for 10 minutes, then drain. This is a very important stage, as it softens the leaves and helps control the salt levels.

To make the filling, place the oil, cinnamon stick and onions in a saucepan. Cook on a medium heat so the onions soften without colouring. When they are translucent, mix in the turmeric, cayenne and dried mint. Add the rice and salt and mix well to coat all over. Pour in the lemon juice and allow to absorb, then add the water and leave to cook until most of the liquid has been absorbed and the onion-rice mixture is sticky. Remove from the pan to a large tray or plate to cool. Once cooled, stir in the fresh mint.

Now it is time to fill the leaves. Lay them on a flat surface with their shiny side down. If there are any little stems, cut them off with scissors as they will be too tough to eat. Top each leaf with a teaspoon of the onion-rice mixture and then fold to make a rice-filled parcel – bring the sides of the leaf over first, then roll it up till you have a small log about the size of your thumb. Continue making vine leaf parcels until you finish all the rice or lose your patience, whichever happens first. Any leftover leaves will be used later to line the cooking pot.

Heat your oven to 180°C/160°C fan/gas mark 4.

Cut the leeks into thick slices (about 2cm wide), break the grapes up into little clusters of 3–5, and wash everything with plenty of water.

Slice the lemon thinly and then choose a small ovenproof pan (20cm diameter) that will contain all the stuffed leaves and cooking ingredients snugly. If you own a thick-bottomed pan, that would be best. Line the base with any leftover or torn leaves and scatter with some slices of lemon and some of the leeks and grapes. Cover with the vine leaf parcels in a tight layer, then top with the rest of the leeks, lemons and grapes and any remaining leaves.

Pour over the lemon juice and olive oil and place the pan on the stove. Bring to the boil, then turn the heat down to a gentle simmer and allow to cook for 5 minutes – this will release some of the liquid from the leeks and grapes. Top up with water so that the leaves are just covered and return to the boil. Place a 20cm disk of greaseproof paper directly on the top of the leaves and cover with the lid, or with aluminium foil.

Place in the centre of the oven and bake for 30 minutes. After this time, remove the lid and paper carefully and check to see how much liquid is left in the pan. If it has mostly disappeared, pull a stuffed vine leaf out and taste it to see if the rice is cooked (be careful, it will be hot). If there is still lots of water in the pan, return it to the oven, increase the heat by 10°C and bake for another 15 minutes.

Allow the stuffed vine leaves to cool in the pan before removing them; this will help them keep their shape. Discard any vine leaves used to line the pan, but keep the cooked leeks, grapes and lemon slices to use as garnish. We like to eat stuffed vine leaves warm, but they are just as nice cold and will keep well in an airtight container in the fridge for a couple of days. We love serving these with goats' yogurt.

Stuffed (wedded) sardines

Mediterranean sardines are delicious but tiny, barely a mouthful each. That could be the reason this dish was invented – two sardines glued together with a paste made of fish roe and herbs, and then fried. The result looks like a couple in coitus, hence the name 'wedded sardines' (this is a dish from North Africa, where coitus means marriage). The sardines we get in this country are just as good but much bigger, so (sadly) there is no need to couple them; they remain single, but still delicious. Ask your fishmonger to butterfly the sardines, or you can do it yourself. If you haven't done it before, I'd suggest that you check online to see how – if I were to try to explain the process here, you would never try it, but it is truly simple.

Dinner for 4

8 medium-sized sardines, butterflied
vegetable oil for frying
flour for coating
a pinch of salt
a pinch of freshly ground black pepper

For the filling
    1 small bunch of coriander (about 15–20g)
    1 small bunch of parsley (about 15–20g)
    1 clove of garlic
    3 anchovy fillets or 1 tbsp salted cod roe

For the potato salad
    1kg potatoes, peeled and diced
    1.5 litres water
    1 tsp salt
    ¼ tsp turmeric
    2 tbsp olive oil
    a pinch of freshly ground black pepper
    2 cloves of garlic, peeled and crushed
    juice of ½ lemon (about 1 tbsp)
    3 tbsp small capers
    3 tbsp chopped parsley
    2 sticks of celery, finely chopped

For the tomato salsa
    4 plum tomatoes, halved
    2 tbsp olive oil
    a generous pinch of salt

To make the filling, simply blitz all the ingredients together. Place a teaspoonful of the filling on the cut surface of each butterflied sardine, spread it all over and then close it up so it looks like a whole fish. Cover the sardines and place in the fridge till you are ready to fry them – this can be done up to a day in advance.

Place the diced potatoes in a large pan with the water, salt and turmeric and bring to the boil. Boil for 6–7 minutes, then check a cube to see if a knife goes thorough it easily and, if it does, quickly drain. Transfer the warm potatoes to a large mixing bowl, add the olive oil, pepper and crushed garlic, and carefully toss around to coat. Set aside for 15–20 minutes to cool, then stir in the remaining ingredients. Adjust the seasoning if needed.

Grate the tomatoes on a coarse grater until you are left with the empty skins. Discard the skins and season the tomato pulp with the olive oil and salt.

Heat a large pan containing 2cm of vegetable oil until very hot. Season some flour with salt and pepper and dip the sardines in it to give them a little coating – this helps the skin go lovely and crispy when fried. Drop a little pinch of flour into the oil to test the heat – it should fizz up immediately. Carefully place the sardines in the hot oil. Don't overfill the pan; it's better to cook these in batches and allow plenty of space for them to crisp up. Fry for 2 minutes on each side, then remove to a plate lined with some kitchen paper to absorb any excess oil.

Once the fish are all fried, sprinkle them very lightly with some sea salt and serve straight away with the potato salad and tomato salsa, preferably on a balcony overlooking the Med.

Mishmishiya

On our quest to find a publisher for this book we fell head-over-heels in love with Alexandra, a charmer and a cab thief with Moroccan heritage, who lives in a houseboat on the River Thames near Chelsea – a very appropriate abode for such a romantic figure. She gave us a pretty little book that she loves and that reminded us of this dish (which is not to be confused with the sweet that goes by a similar name). This recipe works equally well with lamb, beef or mutton, although beef or mutton mince will need a longer cooking time: once the meatballs look done, I eat one to make sure – if it is soft and melts in the mouth, they're ready.

Will make 12 balls in a rich sauce – decide how many people you want to share it with...

For the meatballs
   1 apple, peeled and grated (about 100g)
   1 potato, peeled and grated (about 100g)
   1 onion, peeled and grated (about 100g)
   500g minced lamb
   1 small bunch of coriander, chopped (about 15–20g)
   2 tbsp baharat spice mix (page 12)
   1 tsp salt
   ½ tsp white pepper

For the sauce
   1 tin chopped plum tomatoes (400g)
   120ml water
   1 small bunch of coriander, chopped (about 15–20g)
   4 cloves of garlic, peeled
   1 tsp ground turmeric
   1 tsp ground cardamom pods (page 11)
   1 tsp salt
   200g dried apricots, halved
   1 orange, sliced with the skin on

Place all the sauce ingredients except the apricots and orange slices in a food processor and purée till smooth.

Preheat the oven to 220°C/200°C fan/gas mark 7.

Squeeze out any excess juice from the grated apple, potato and onion and mix with the minced lamb, chopped coriander, spice mix, salt and pepper. Form into twelve balls, each roughly the size of a golf ball (about 60g). Set them in a large pan or a deep roasting tray that is big enough to accommodate them all in one layer and roast in the oven for 15 minutes.

Add the sauce, orange slices and apricots to the meatballs and return to the oven. Lower the temperature to 200°C/180°C fan/gas mark 6 and cook for 30 minutes. Then remove carefully and mix well, cover and return to the oven. Reduce the heat to 180°C/160°C fan/gas mark 4 and continue cooking for a further 40 minutes.

Serve with some white rice, couscous or just a loaf of bread.

Makshi – stuffed peppers with beef & rice

With most of the dishes in this book we ask ourselves: 'Will Cornelia cook this?' We always have a terrific time in Cornelia and Peter's West London flat – she says it's Ladbroke Grove but actually it's closer to Latimer Road. She is an adventurous cook and a terrific hostess with very high standards, and is constantly on the lookout for new, exotic dishes to cook at her dinner parties. We know that recipes that pass the 'Cornelia test' are keepers. This dish has no exotic spicing, no fireworks of flavour, but it is honest, humble and as good as a cuddle. A great one to cook for a lot of people you don't need to impress, just nourish.

Dinner for 4 (we allow 2 peppers per person for a main meal)

8 small red peppers
1 lemon, sliced
1 tomato, sliced

For the filling
1 large onion, peeled and finely diced (about 150g)
4 cloves of garlic, peeled and crushed
2 tbsp olive oil
250g minced beef
2 tsp salt
2 tsp ground pimento (allspice)
2 tsp paprika
2 tsp ground cumin
½ tsp cayenne pepper
90g long-grain rice (we use Tilda Basmati)
2 tomatoes, diced (about 200g)
1 small bunch of parsley (about 15–20g), leaves chopped (keep the stalks for cooking)

For the cooking liquor
70g tomato purée
3 bay leaves
4 whole cloves of garlic, peeled
about 1 litre water

Run a knife around the top of each pepper, about 1cm below the stalk, and pull the top section off. Trim the seeds and pith from inside the pepper tops. Set the tops aside to use as lids for the filled peppers later. Remove the seeds and any white membrane from inside the peppers.

Set the cleaned peppers upright in a pan that can contain them sitting really snugly side-by-side. Wedge the lemon and tomato slices all around them to hold them in place. You can also push all the parsley stalks in around them for added flavour.

Fry the onion and garlic in the oil over a medium heat until softened, then add the minced beef, breaking it up as it fries until it has all changed colour and gone crumbly. Sprinkle in the salt and spices and mix well, then tip in the rice and fry for a minute. Finally add the tomato dice and the chopped parsley. Remove from the heat and mix to combine. Spoon the mince and rice mixture into the peppers to fill them. Don't squash it in too firmly, as the rice will puff up as it cooks.

Put the cooking liquor ingredients in a saucepan and bring to the boil. Pour over the filled peppers, letting some liquid go into each one. Cover each pepper with a pepper lid (it's a bit like a puzzle to fit the lids) and place the pepper pan on a high heat. Once the liquid is boiling, cover the pan and reduce the heat to cook on a slow simmer for 30 minutes.

Check how much liquid is left in the pan (it should be about three-quarters full – if it looks a little low, top up with some more water). Baste the peppers with the cooking liquor and re-cover the pan. Simmer for a further 20 minutes, then serve, or keep for the next day – these improve with time. You can reheat them in a microwave or do as I do and nibble them cold.

Meatballs with peas, mint & yogurt

The perfume rising from this pot is enough to transport you to a dreamland Persia, all minarets, walled gardens and soft silk slippers. It is also perfect for British springtime: green-tasting and light, but still hearty enough to dispel the cold damp outside.

Makes 12 balls (you'll need 3 balls each, but will want a 4th)

For the meatballs
1 large potato, peeled and grated (about 250g)
400g minced lamb
250g minced beef
1 small onion, finely diced (about 120g)
1 small bunch of coriander, chopped (about 10g)
1 small bunch of fresh mint, chopped (about 15g)
1 tsp ground turmeric
1 tsp ground cumin
1 tsp ground pimento (allspice)
1 tsp salt
½ tsp white pepper
1 egg

For the cooking liquor
1 tbsp olive oil
1 large onion, diced (about 150g)
4 cloves of garlic, peeled and cracked with the flat of your knife
1 tsp salt
2 whole dried Persian lemons, cut in half
1 small dried red chilli, cracked in half
½ cinnamon stick
1 litre water

To finish
250g natural yogurt
1 egg yolk
4 tsp dried mint
1 tbsp cornflour
200g shelled peas (fresh or frozen)
fresh mint leaves, or pea shoots if you can get some, to garnish

Heat your oven to 200°C/180°C fan/gas mark 6.

Squeeze out any excess liquid from the grated potato (you should end up with about 150g) and mix in a large bowl with all the other meatball ingredients. Form the mixture into twelve balls of roughly 60g each. Place on a lightly-oiled baking tray and bake in the centre of the oven for 10 minutes.

While the meatballs are baking, place a large saucepan on a medium-high heat and add the olive oil, onion, garlic and salt. Sauté until the onion starts to soften. Add the Persian lemons, chilli and cinnamon stick and fry together for one minute, then pour in the water and bring to the boil.

Remove the meatballs from the oven and add to the boiling cooking liquor. Return to the boil, then reduce the heat to a constant simmer and cook slowly for 45 minutes. You can prepare up to this stage in advance – the meatballs and cooking liquor will keep for a day or two in an airtight container in the fridge. Then when you want to finish making the dish, simply tip the meatballs and liquor into a large pan and bring to a simmer for about 10 minutes to heat through thoroughly before continuing with the rest of the recipe.

Mix the yogurt in a bowl with the egg yolk, dried mint and cornflour until fully combined.

If you are using fresh peas, add them to the simmering meatballs, increase the heat and cook for 3 minutes; if you are using frozen peas, just pop them in – they won't need any additional cooking time. Then, stirring carefully all the while, add the yogurt mixture to the meatball liquor. Return to the boil and cook for one minute to thicken the sauce.

Serve straight away, sprinkling some fresh mint leaves and/or pea shoots onto each dish to garnish. This dish is great on its own, but it will also work beautifully with fragrant basmati or jasmine rice.

If you have any meatballs left over, they will keep for a day or two in the fridge. Reheat them thoroughly on a low heat with a spoonful of water to loosen up the sauce or pop them into the microwave.

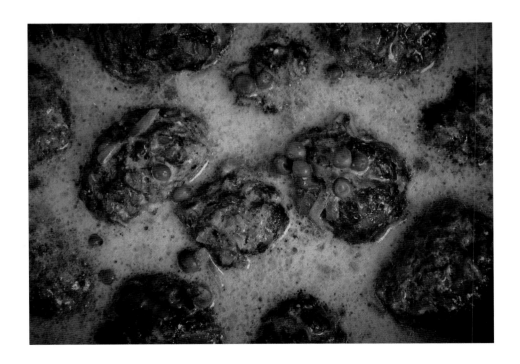

Meatballs in a sweet, sour & spicy tomato sauce

This started its life as *mafrum*, a traditional dish from Tunisia that is notoriously tortuous to make. The chosen vegetable victim is prepped, stuffed, battered, fried and then cooked in a sauce. Even for Sarit, who loves fiddly things, creating pockets out of potatoes and quinces proved too much. In this version we cut out the stuffing, battering and frying but leave in everything that matters, so it's almost all pleasure, no pain. You will need a whole large garlic bulb for this recipe; it looks a lot but is well worth it.

Makes 12 balls with plenty of delicious sauce

For the meatballs
250g minced lamb
250g minced beef
1 large onion, peeled and grated (about 200g)
2 cloves of garlic, peeled and grated or finely chopped
30g (2 tbsp) breadcrumbs
1 tsp smoky paprika
½ tsp chilli flakes or cayenne pepper
1 tsp harissa paste (or Turkish acı biber salçası, if you can get hold of it)
½ tsp salt
a pinch of white pepper
a pinch of ground cinnamon

For the sauce
2 tbsp olive oil
the rest of the head of garlic, peeled and chopped (about 30g)
½ tsp salt
5 tbsp tomato purée (about 80g)
1 tbsp harissa paste (or Turkish acı biber salçası, if you can get hold of it)
1 tsp smoky paprika
½ cinnamon stick
2 bay leaves
1 tbsp Demerara sugar
2 strips of lemon skin (use a peeler)
100ml lemon juice
750ml water
2 large pears or quinces (in season), cut in thick wedges, seeds removed but skin on (it helps them keep their shape while cooking)

Heat your oven to 200°C/180°C fan/gas mark 6.

Mix all the meatball ingredients together in a large bowl and form into twelve balls of roughly 50g each. Place on a lightly oiled baking tray in the centre of the oven and bake for 15 minutes.

While the meatballs are cooking, put the olive oil, chopped garlic and salt in a large saucepan on a medium-high heat and fry for about 2 minutes, stirring all the while, until a strong garlicky smell emerges and the garlic begins to stick to the pan (it should not colour). Add the tomato purée, harissa, spices, bay leaves, sugar and lemon skin and mix well. Keep stirring and cooking until everything begins to stick to the bottom of the pan again (about 4–5 minutes), then stir in the lemon juice and bring to the boil. Once it is boiling, pour in the water, stir well and bring back to the boil.

By now your meatballs should be just about ready to jump into the sauce. Tip them in along with all the juices that have come out of them – there's tons of flavour there. If you are using quinces, add them at the same time as the meatballs. Bring the sauce to the boil again, then reduce the heat to a minimum, cover and leave to cook slowly for an hour.

If you are using pears, add them now. Cook for 15 minutes on a low heat without the lid in order to reduce the liquid slightly – when it's ready, the sauce should resemble a thick soup.

We like to serve this dish with white rice, couscous or some lovely soft bread like milk bun (page 67).

Balls & Stuff.

Dushpra – cherries, lamb & sweet spice dumplings

Original *dushpra* is a soup flavoured with cherries and lamb, with tiny dumplings floating in it. We loved the flavours but making the little dumplings would take up all our time. We decided to super-size the dumplings and turn this into a main course. It is still heinously time-consuming and fiddly, but it is a true stunner, and is the only dish I know that will stretch one lamb shank to feed four, and do it with incredible style.

Makes 16 dumplings. Will serve 4 if you are good, fewer if you are greedy.

For the dumpling dough
200g '00' flour
½ tsp salt
1 egg
40g soft butter
about 60ml water

For the braised shank
1 large lamb shank (550g at least)
½ onion, skin and all
2 cloves of garlic, unpeeled
2 star anise
1 cinnamon stick
2 tsp sweet spice mix (page 12)
½ tsp salt
2 tbsp sour cherry jam
    (or you can use raspberry)

For the filling
all the cooked lamb (about 180g–200g)
30g dried sour cherries, roughly chopped
½ tsp sweet spice mix (page 12)
3 sprigs of mint, picked and chopped

For the sauce
100g cooked chickpeas (from 40g dried,
    or use tinned)
12 cherries, halved and stoned
fresh mint or tarragon leaves (to finish)

Start by making the dough – mix the flour with the salt, egg and soft butter, then add a teaspoon of water at a time until it all comes together to a nice smooth dough. Cover it with cling film and keep in the fridge for later.

Place the lamb shank in a large pan with all the other braising ingredients and cover with water. Bring to the boil and skim any foam that comes to the top. Reduce the heat to a constant simmer, cover and cook for about 1½ hours until the meat comes away from the bone easily. Strain and retain all the cooking liquid, pick out all the meat and discard the rest.

Put the cooking liquid back in the pan, add the chickpeas and set on the stove to simmer uncovered until reduced by half. This will be the sauce for your dumplings later on.

Shred the meat and mix it with the other filling ingredients. Taste and check for salt – you may want to add a pinch. Roll the dough as thinly as you can; if you have a pasta machine it would work well for this, but I usually just do it by hand as then I can roll the whole amount at once. Try to keep the dough in a square shape, so that you have no trimmings or waste.

Cut the dough into a 4x4 grid of squares, each about the size of a drinks coaster (about 6cm square), and divide the lamb filling evenly between them, so that you have a little heap in the centre of each one. Brush the edges of the dough with a little water (to help them stick), fold each square corner-to-corner into a triangle to cover the filling and press down the edges to seal. I like to then take the two outer corners, fold them around my finger and pinch together, so that they look like little tortellini.

Boil a large pot of salted water and drop the dumplings in for 3 minutes. Then transfer them to the reduced stock and add the cherries. Heat together for a minute or two to warm through, then serve with fresh mint or tarragon leaves on top.

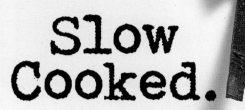

Slow
Cooked.

We try not to hire professional chefs, or at least not very experienced ones. Perhaps we are being unfair, but we know that a lifetime of feeding people can make chefs a bit careless, a bit callous with food, and we want our food to be handled with the care of a home cook feeding loved ones. So rather than skill, we are looking for heart. Sometimes (rarely) this policy works.

Giorgia was the first one to join; a cake fanatic, she treats pastry like it's a martial art – seriously, with fierce determination. We were very lucky to find Julia (she says she found us), whose heart is as great as her skills and who has a palate to match; she now runs our kitchen with Polish determination and her unique cheer.

We thought we had struck gold when we found Aristo, a bespectacled Spaniard with a winning smile who loves to eat, loves to cook and loves to feed people. He loved our food too, and wanted to learn so much that we could not foresee any problem. Our assumption has always been that if someone really wants to do the job, they can do the job; however, we did not take into account chronic clumsiness, a panicky disposition and a complete inability to retain information from one day to the next. Our kitchen became a warzone as Aristo trailed through it, bumping into equipment and furniture, leaving spillages and all kinds of debris in his wake. We soon realised that we could not leave him alone for a second, or if we did we would find ourselves with preparations so different from what we had wanted, we could not even tell what he was attempting to make. But we felt he was genuinely trying, and we liked him too much to let him go. We thought he could do the routine jobs, the repetitive tasks that are the backbone of every kitchen: slicing radishes, picking and washing parsley, picking pomegranate seeds. After a semi-successful week he graduated to cooking the lamb. This involves marinating it after lunch service; placing it in trays lined with aromatics, pink plums and roses; later, towards the tail-end of dinner service, putting it all in the deck oven (the stones in it as hot as can be after a whole day's work); letting it all brown a bit, then putting a lid on it, turning the oven off and leaving it to cook in the residual heat all night. In the morning our noses would tell us how Aristo had done before we even got to the kitchen. We learned to recognise the different scenarios – an acrid smell meant he had left the oven on; steam meant he had forgotten to put the lid on; BBQ smell meant he had forgotten to add any liquid; and no smell at all meant that the lamb was still in the fridge, resting on its cold, pretty bed, and off the menu for today.

But if everything had gone to plan, the smell that welcomed us in the morning was pure joy: browned meat and vegetables roasting, sweet and sour caramel from the plums, a background perfume of roses and rose water – a promise of a true feast for everyone who came to eat with us that day, and a return of faith in our team and humanity, and our hiring policy.

These recipes are intended to give maximum value for minimum effort. All you need is a piece of meat (not an expensive one), the flavouring of your choice, some vegetables and a few hours in the oven. The result will be tender, flavoursome meat that will bring with it some sauce and a hit of nostalgia, a kind of sweet homesickness, even if you are already home.

Slow-cooked lamb shoulder with plums & roses

This dish looks as girly as can be – the bed of pink plums and rose petals makes it look like the set of a lingerie shoot or perfume commercial – but the flavours are grown-up and complex, and should appeal to both sexes.

For 4–6 for a festive blowout evening

1 lamb shoulder, on the bone
1 celeriac
2 heads of garlic
12 red plums
1 tbsp sugar
3 tbsp dried rose petals, plus more to garnish
2 large cinnamon sticks
2 glasses of white wine
chopped soft, fragrant herbs (coriander/ parsley/mint/chervil, etc.), to garnish

For the marinade
1 large onion
1 tbsp ground cardamom pods (page 11)
2 tbsp ground coriander
1 tbsp dried rose petals
1 tbsp ground cinnamon
2 tsp salt
½ tsp white pepper

Use a food processor or a pestle and mortar to purée the marinade ingredients together to a paste. Rub all over the lamb shoulder and leave to sit for about an hour at room temperature to allow the lamb and marinade to get acquainted.

Preheat your oven to 250°C/230°C fan/gas mark 9.

Peel the celeriac and cut into chunky cubes. Break the garlic into cloves but don't peel. Quarter 8 of the plums. Cut the remaining 4 plums into wedges, place in a bowl, sprinkle with the sugar and set aside till later.

Place the celeriac, garlic, quartered plums, rose petals and cinnamon sticks in a large, deep roasting tray and place the marinated lamb on top. Put the tray uncovered in the centre of the oven for 30 minutes, by which time the lamb should have started to colour and brown (it may take another 10 minutes if your oven doesn't run very hot).

Pour the wine into the tray and leave to cook for another 15 minutes, then pour in enough water to reach halfway up the lamb joint. Cover the tray with aluminium foil. Lower the oven temperature to 200°C/180°C fan/gas mark 6 and cook for 1 hour.

Remove the roasting tray from the oven, baste the lamb with the liquid at the bottom of the tray, then re-cover and return to the oven. Reduce the heat to 180°C/160°C fan/gas mark 5 and cook for a further hour, basting halfway through this time and again when the hour is up. Then add the plum wedges that you kept aside and return the covered tray to the oven for the final 30–45 minutes. The meat should be falling off the bone.

Preferably serve in the roasting tray, with some rose petals and chopped herbs sprinkled on top of the lamb for show, and a mound of buttered rice or couscous alongside, to soak up the sauce.

Sofrito

Sofrito is the signature dish of Jerusalem, my home town. The name comes from the *ladino* dialect, a kind of pidgin Spanish spoken by the oldest Jewish community there. To me *sofrito* is the essence of the simple, no-frills, salt-and-pepper cooking typical of this town. The meat is browned slowly in its own fat, then a ton of onions are browned in that same fat. Potatoes are added along with seasonal variations – artichokes, Jerusalem artichokes, turnips, quince... A few tomatoes or tomato purée can be added for colour and sweetness; plums or prunes are another option. All this is left to cook in a large pot on the lowest flame for a few hours or overnight. Inside the pot the meat and vegetables release their juices and slowly stew in them. These juices later reduce into a thick, glistening, savoury glaze. The resulting meat is utterly melting and somehow tastes meatier than usual, but the main events for me are always the potatoes – lacquered and soft, browned to the core by the juice of meat and onion – and the scent, which for me is the essential smell of home.

Short ribs with dates, date molasses & potatoes

Serves 2, with leftovers

3 tbsp vegetable oil
850g beef short ribs
2 tsp sea salt
½ tsp freshly ground black pepper
2 onions, peeled (about 350g)
2 potatoes, peeled (about 450g)
1 tbsp tomato purée
60g dried pitted dates
120ml water
2 tbsp date molasses, to glaze

Heat the oil in a large frying pan on a high heat. Place the short ribs flat-side down in the pan and season with the salt and pepper. Allow to brown on one side before turning and colouring the other side (about 3–4 minutes on each). In the meantime, cut each onion into six wedges and each potato into eight wedges.

Remove the ribs from the frying pan and place in a large ovenproof pot, leaving the frying pan on the heat. Put the onions in the frying pan and allow to colour a little (keep the heat high) – this will take about 2–3 minutes. Then add the potato wedges and cook for a further 2 minutes. Add the tomato purée and stir around to coat the vegetables, then tip the contents of the frying pan on top of the meat in the ovenproof pot.

Add the dates and water, cover the pot and cook – you can either simmer it on a very low heat for a very long time (3–4 hours), or do as we do and place it in the oven at 160°C/140°C fan/gas mark 3 for 3–4 hours, or, even better, set your oven to 150°C/130°C fan/gas mark 2 and let it cook very slowly overnight. The potatoes will brown and caramelise and the meat will become very tender and fall off the bone. Before serving, brush the meat with the date molasses to make it shiny and sweet. Perfect.

Ox cheeks with quince & bay leaf

Quince is the most fragrant, flavourful of fruit. We are so mad for it that when the season starts, you can have a three-course meal at Honey & Co with quince in every course and accompany it with quince and cinnamon iced tea (page 273). We have roasted, poached, braised, jammed and stuffed it, and still get excited about finding new ways with it. The greatest joy, however, is burying your face in a bowl of heavy, ripe fruit and getting high on the smell.

Dinner for 4

2–3 cleaned ox cheeks (about 1 kg) – get
  your butcher to prep them for you

For the salt rub
  3 tsp sea salt
  1 tsp cumin seeds
  a pinch of black pepper
  2 bay leaves

For cooking
  2 tbsp vegetable oil (or beef dripping,
    if you have it)
  1 litre water
  1 carrot, peeled and slit in half lengthways
  3 celery sticks
  2 large quinces, cored (but not peeled)
    and cut in 6–8 wedges
  1 cinnamon stick
  1 head of garlic, cut in half across the bulb
    to expose all cloves
  4 bay leaves
  1 tsp cumin seeds

Grind the salt rub ingredients together roughly using a pestle and mortar, or just crush them together with a wooden spoon. Sprinkle generously all over the ox cheeks, place in a bowl, cover and set in the fridge for 2–3 hours to let the salt draw out the impurities. You cannot skip this stage.

Lift the cheeks out of the liquid that will have been produced and pat them dry with kitchen paper.

Heat the oil in a frying pan over a high heat and place the cheeks in it. Allow them about 2 minutes on each side to colour and sear, then remove to a braising tray (basically any ovenproof pan or tray with a lid). Pour a litre of water into the frying pan and scrape up all the goodness with a flat wooden spoon. Bring to the boil, then pour over the ox cheeks.

Add all the other ingredients to the braising tray and, if need be, top up the water so that it covers the contents entirely. Place in the oven at 180°C/160°C fan/gas mark 4 and braise for 2 hours (or you could cook it on the stove on a very slow simmer for the same length of time). Check that the meat is really soft, then allow to cool in the liquid.

Serve with bulgar wheat or couscous (or a lovely alternative is to add 90g of *freekeh* to the pot for the last hour of cooking, so that it absorbs all the delicious juices).

Oxtail sofrito

This is far from traditional but works so well, with the sweet potatoes caramelising and adding sweetness, and the oranges adding another tone altogether. The best thing is that the actual preparation time is only 10 minutes; then cooking for 5–6 hours will produce a real treat.

Dinner for 4–6

3 tbsp vegetable oil
1 oxtail, cut into thick pieces (about 1.5kg)
2 large sweet potatoes, peeled and cut into large chunks (about 800g)
2 onions, peeled and each cut into 6 wedges (about 220g)
6–8 cloves of garlic, unpeeled
1 orange, thickly sliced (skin and all)
juice of 2 oranges

Preheat your oven to 220°C/200°C fan/ gas mark 7.

Heat the oil in a large ovenproof pan over a high heat and place the oxtail pieces in it. Season generously with salt and pepper and cook for 2–3 minutes. Turn the pieces over with a pair of tongs, season the other side and allow another 2–3 minutes cooking. Add the sweet potatoes, onions, garlic and orange slices, and push everything in so that the vegetables and fruit are wedged between pieces of meat. Pour in the orange juice and allow to boil, then cover the pan and place in the centre of the oven for 1 hour.

Reduce the heat to 200°C/180°C fan/gas mark 6 and cook for another hour, then reduce it again, this time to 160°C/140°C fan/gas mark 4, and leave to cook for a further 2–3 hours.

Check carefully – the meat should pull off the bone easily. Serve with a fresh side salad.

Patlican - lamb & aubergine stew

You can tell all you need to know about a restaurant by the food it serves the staff. One place I worked at was famous for its 'staff gratin' – all the leftovers and offcuts from the day before baked in a dish under a heavy blanket of cheap cheese. Another restaurant would buy in ready-made beef pies for 13 pence a piece – I dread to think what kind of meat cost so little; certainly not beef. In Moro, one of the best restaurants in the world, everybody eats together between services, and the staff lunch there is better than the food that most restaurants serve their customers. This dish was the highlight of our staff meal repertoire in a restaurant I worked for in Israel. Moosh, a gifted comedian and cook of Turkish origin, would freeze the trimmings from all the lamb we butchered and, when we had accumulated enough, would make this dish for us. I think it is the only time I took staff food home with me to share with my wife – the lamb and aubergine combine to make something really special. This is not the best-looking dish, as it is brown and sludgy. Do not cook it to impress. Cook it for the ones you love most, or just for you; it is that good.

Dinner for 2

450g lamb neck, cut into large dice
½ tsp salt
½ tsp freshly ground black pepper
1 tbsp olive oil
1 aubergine, cut into large cubes (about 350g)
1 large tomato, cut into large cubes (about 120g)
1 small red onion, peeled and cut into wedges (about 100g)
6 whole cloves of garlic, peeled
¼ – ½ small red chilli, thinly sliced
3 sprigs of fresh thyme
150ml water
1 tbsp pomegranate molasses

Season the lamb cubes with the salt and pepper. Heat a large pan over a medium-high heat, add the olive oil and diced lamb, and sear the meat all over. Once it has browned (after about 5–6 minutes), add the aubergine, tomato, onion and garlic. Cover the pan and leave to steam for 5 minutes, then remove the lid, mix everything around and add the chilli and thyme. Reduce the heat to low and cook slowly for about 15 minutes before pouring in the water and pomegranate molasses. Continue cooking on a low heat for 50–60 minutes until all the vegetables have broken down and the meat is so soft you can tear it apart with your fork.

This is best eaten straight from the pot with a spoon, at the kitchen counter or in front of the TV. Bread is definitely required.

Octopus in meshwiya sauce with celery salad

This has been an unlikely star of our menu and a constant best-seller, so much so that we struggle to take it off the menu. I had never realised that Londoners have such an appetite for octopus. Cooking it requires no special equipment or skill, and minimal attention, so it's nothing to be nervous about. The octopus cooks in its own briny juices which will make it really tender without losing any of the flavour, as happens when you steam or boil it. Frozen octopods are easy to find and are better than fresh, as the freezing helps to tenderise them. If you do get a fresh one, you will need to bash it against a wall repeatedly for 10 minutes or so, then hang it on a washing line in the sun to tenderise, as they do in Greece. This method may damage your wall paint and the general cleanliness of your home, plus it may tire your arm and shoulder. Better perhaps to freeze the beast for a few hours and defrost it later. We like to serve this dish with a fresh, light celery salad.

Makes 4 light main course portions, or an excellent starter for 6

For the octopus
1 large octopus, defrosted (about 1.5–1.8kg before cooking)
1 small leek, cut in 3 large pieces
3 stalks of celery, cut in 3 pieces
2 tsp whole coriander seeds
2 tsp whole fennel seeds
1 tsp whole black peppercorns
60ml white wine
2 tbsp olive oil

For the meshwiya sauce
1 large red pepper
3 plum tomatoes
¼ tsp salt
1 tbsp + 1 tbsp olive oil
1 tsp whole caraway seeds
1 tsp whole cumin seeds
3 cloves of garlic, peeled
3 sprigs of coriander, picked and chopped

For the celery salad
3 light green inner sticks of celery
1 lemon
3 sprigs of coriander
1 tbsp olive oil
¼ tsp salt

Preheat the oven to 240°C/220°C fan/ gas mark 9.

Place all the ingredients for cooking the octopus bar the olive oil in a large pan with a lid, cover and cook in the centre of the oven for 30 minutes. Remove from the oven and open the lid carefully; there will be clouds of steam, as the octopus will have let out a large amount of water. Stir well and try to make sure as much of the octopus as possible is submerged, then re-cover and return to the oven. Lower the heat to 200°C/180°C fan/gas mark 6 and cook for another 30 minutes. Remove from the oven again, stir and re-submerge the octopus, then re-cover and return to the oven to cook for a further 30 minutes, this time at 180°C/160°C fan/gas mark 4.

Insert a small knife into one of the thick tentacles – it should go in easily. If it feels rubbery, return the pan to the oven for another 10 minutes or so before checking again. Once tender, remove from the oven and leave to cool in the pan.

When it is cool enough to handle, remove the octopus from the cooking liquid and place on a chopping board. Remove the small cap and scrape out any impurities from inside, then cut it into rings that resemble calamari and place these in a bowl. In the middle of the beast where all the legs connect is the beak, a small hard ball which is easily removed with a knife. Discard this. Next are the tentacles: separate them from each other and cut each in half. You should now have a thin end bit and a thicker top bit – cut the thicker one down its length so that all the pieces are more or less the same size. Place in a bowl with the other pieces and coat them in the olive oil. You can prepare this stage a day in advance if you want – just cover and keep in the fridge until you are ready to fry it.

If you are preparing the octopus and the *meshwiya* sauce on the same day, you can put the vegetables in to roast when the octopus goes in for its first 30 minutes in the oven. Otherwise, if you've prepared the octopus in advance, preheat the oven to 240°C/220°C fan/gas mark 9.

Quarter the pepper and remove the seeds and any white pith. Cut into roughly 1cm cubes and place in a roasting pan. Cut each tomato into 4–5 thick slices and add to the peppers. Sprinkle with the salt and 1 tablespoon of olive oil and roast in the oven for 30 minutes. Allow to cool, then chop finely.

Lower the heat to 200°C/180°C fan/gas mark 6, roast the caraway and cumin on a tray for 3 minutes, and allow to cool. You can do this in the same oven as the octopus while it is cooking for its second 30 minutes, if you're preparing sauce and octopus on the same day. Crush the roasted seeds using a pestle and mortar, or chop them finely with a knife.

Chop the garlic as finely as you can and mix in a bowl with the chopped roasted vegetables and crushed seeds, Add the second tablespoon of olive oil and the chopped coriander. Stir well to combine. You can make this sauce a day in advance too – just refrigerate until you are ready to cook.

Peel the celery to remove the stringy parts, then cut into thin slices and place in a bowl. Reserve a few celery leaves to garnish. Cut the lemon in half. Juice one half into the bowl and cut the other half into the thinnest slices possible. Add the lemon slices to the bowl. Pick the leaves off the coriander and add them too, as well as the oil and the salt. Mix well.

When you are ready to assemble the dish, set a large frying pan on a high heat, add the octopus along with the olive oil that was covering it and fry for 6–7 minutes, allowing the octopus pieces to heat up and caramelise.

Spread the *meshwiya* sauce on individual plates and top with the hot octopus. Spoon the celery salad all over, add a few celery leaves onto each plate and serve.

Musakhan

A mutual friend brought Ash to the restaurant. He liked us and loved this dish, and we liked him a lot. On that first visit he declared himself our 'second cousin, once removed', and every time he comes, it's a great joy. In his opinion, we have yet to prepare a chicken dish, or any dish for that matter, that is better than this one, and he doesn't understand why we don't keep it on the menu always. Every so often, when we feel it's been too long, we will drop him a line, saying, 'Hi cuz, we are making your chicken dish,' and he will always come to eat it, and take some home. He is not the only fan; this dish is such a great thing to eat – a crispy bread parcel with juicy chicken inside, and plenty of sauce. The little salad is a real gem too, a prettier take on the classic kebab shop salad.

**Serves 4
as a generous
main course**

For the filling
8 chicken thighs with skin and bones
  (about 1kg)
1 tsp + 1 tsp salt
3 large onions, peeled and thinly sliced
  (about 450g)
1 whole dried chilli (you can shake the
  seeds out to make the filling milder)
100g dried currants
80g pomegranate molasses
240ml water

For the parcel
1 packet of thin Lebanese flat bread or
  tortilla wraps (4–8 wraps, depending
  on thickness)
a little olive oil, for brushing

For the salad
2 small red onions, peeled and sliced as
  thinly as possible (about 150g)
1 tsp sumac (or juice of 1 lemon)
seeds from 1 pomegranate
1 large bunch of parsley, picked
  (about 30–40g)
a pinch of sea salt
1 tbsp olive oil

Preheat the oven to 200°C/180°C fan/ gas mark 6.

Put a large heavy-bottomed skillet on a medium heat. Place the chicken thighs skin-side down in it and season with a teaspoon of salt. Allow them to slowly cook and render out all the fat from the skin. This will take about 10–15 minutes and the skin should go all crisp and golden. Flip the chicken pieces and cook for 5 minutes on the other side, then remove them to a large roasting pan.

Add the onions and the other teaspoon of salt to that same skillet and cook on a medium heat until the onions start to soften and colour. Add the dried chilli, currants and pomegranate molasses and mix to coat. Pour over the chicken and add 240ml of water. Cover the roasting pan and cook in the centre of the oven for 1 hour. Check that the flesh comes away easily from the bone and leave to cool.

When the chicken is at a temperature you can handle, pull the meat off the bones and shred into bite-sized pieces. We like to keep bits of skin in the mixture as they are little flavour bombs, but you may prefer to discard them. Discard the dried chilli, then return the meat to the roasted onion and currant mixture and stir to combine. You can make up to this stage in advance and keep it covered in the fridge for a day or two.

Place a flat bread or wrap in a soup bowl, leaving lots of overhang (if it is very thin, use two to make a double layer). Fill the bread with a quarter of the chicken filling, then fold the edges on top to seal like a package. Flip the bowl onto a lined baking tray so that the parcel sits on it seam-side down. Repeat another three times until you have four lovely parcels. Brush them with a little olive oil and place in the oven at 200°C/180°C fan/gas mark 6. It will take about 10–15 minutes until the parcels go crisp and golden.

Mix all the salad ingredients together in a bowl. Serve one parcel per person with a bit of salad on the side. If you're sharing this meal with people you're comfortable with, you can do away with cutlery and eat with your hands – just grab the parcel and sink your teeth in, pinching bits of salad every now and then.

Madfunia

We wanted something festive for the holidays. Turkey was not an option (and should never be, in our opinion). We thought of the grand Moroccan party dish that is called sometimes *shaariya medfouna*, a rich tagine buried under a mound of buttered noodles. Our tagine not only had chestnuts and sultanas but all the sweet spice of Christmas and a fancy hat made of crunchy *kadaif* pastry, to leave no one in any doubt as to what time of year it was.

Serves 4 generously as a main course

For the filling
8 chicken thighs with skin and bones (about 1kg)
1 tsp + 1 tsp salt
3 large onions, peeled and thinly sliced (about 400g)
6 cloves of garlic, peeled and halved lengthways
250g pre-cooked whole chestnuts
100g golden raisins
1 tsp white pepper
2 tsp ground cumin
1 tsp ground cinnamon
1 cinnamon stick
1 tsp cayenne pepper
3 tbsp date molasses or honey
240ml water

To serve
100g kadaif pastry
1 tbsp olive oil

Preheat your oven to 200°C/180°C fan/ gas mark 6.

Put a large heavy-bottomed skillet on a medium heat. Place the chicken thighs skin-side down in it and season with a teaspoon of salt. Allow them to slowly cook and render out all the fat from the skin. This will take about 10–15 minutes and the skin should go all crisp and golden (don't be tempted to steal a bit). Flip the chicken pieces and cook for 5 minutes on the other side, then remove them to a large roasting pan, reserving all the oil and sticky bits in the skillet.

Add the onions, garlic and the other teaspoon of salt to the skillet and cook on a medium heat until the onions and garlic start to soften and colour. In the meantime, break the chestnuts up a little and scatter over the chicken, then sprinkle the raisins all over.

When the onions and garlic are soft, tip in all the spices and mix to coat. Cook for 1 minute while stirring, then add the date molasses or honey and 240ml of water. Bring to the boil and pour over the chicken, chestnuts and raisins.

Cover the roasting pan and cook in the centre of the oven for 1 hour, then turn the heat off and leave the pan inside for an extra 30 minutes while the flavours combine. Remove from the oven and leave to cool.

When the chicken is at a temperature you can handle, break each thigh in half and remove the bone. Set the meat in an ovenproof serving dish and pour over all the lovely cooking juices, onions, raisins and chestnuts. You can prepare up to this point in advance. Once cooled, simply cover and keep in the fridge for a day or two.

Preheat the oven to 200°C/180°C fan/gas mark 6.

Top the chicken mixture in the serving dish with the *kadaif* pastry and drizzle with the olive oil. Place on the upper-middle shelf of the oven for 20–30 minutes to crisp up the pastry. It should go a lovely golden colour.

Bring to the table in the baking dish, divide up and serve with a spoon. Forget about turkey forever.

Chicken pastilla

Serve this with a big plate of orange slices and rocket drizzled in lemon juice and olive oil, and with great pride.

To serve 4 shameless or 6 polite guests

6 chicken thighs with skin and bones
(about 800g)
1 tsp + 1 tsp salt
1 tsp pepper
100g pitted dates
3 onions, peeled and sliced thinly
(about 300g)
1 cinnamon stick
1 dried red chilli (you can remove the seeds
if you prefer milder flavours)
2 tbsp ras el hanut spice mix
240ml water
1 packet of filo pastry (about 250–270g)
60g melted butter (or oil / other fat if
avoiding dairy)

Heat your oven to 200°C/180°C fan/gas mark 6.

Put a large frying pan on a medium heat. Place the chicken thighs skin-side down in it and sprinkle with 1 teaspoon of salt and the pepper. You won't need to add any oil to cook it in, as the skin will render a lot of fat. Keep it on a medium heat and allow the skin to crisp and colour. This will take about 10–15 minutes. Once the skin is all crisp and golden, flip the thighs and cook on the other side for 5 minutes, then use tongs to remove them to an ovenproof pan that is large enough contain them all in one layer. Add the pitted dates.

Keep the fat in the frying pan and add the sliced onions and the other teaspoon of salt. Cook the onions until they are soft and starting to go golden. Add the cinnamon stick, dried chilli and ras el hanut spice and mix well. Cook for 30 seconds, then add the water and bring to the boil. Once boiling, pour over the chicken thighs in the ovenproof pan. Cover the pan and place in the centre of the oven to cook for 1 hour.

Open the lid carefully and check whether the chicken is fully cooked – it should just fall off the bone. If it is still a little tough, cook for a further 10–15 minutes. Set aside until cool enough to handle.

Carefully pour the contents of the pan into a sieve over a bowl. Retain the cooking liquid. Pull the chicken from the bones, discarding them along with any cartilage. Remove the chilli and the cinnamon stick. Mix the chicken meat together with the cooked dates and onions, along with just enough liquid to bind the mixture well – any remaining liquid can be kept to warm through and use as extra sauce when serving. You can prepare this chicken-date-onion mixture up to 2 days in advance. Store in the fridge until you are ready to assemble the pastilla.

Preheat your oven to 200°C/180°C fan/gas mark 6.

Lay the opened packet of filo pastry on the table. Carefully peel off the first sheet and use a brush to butter it, then fold into four and set aside (this folded square will give a thicker base to the *pastilla*). Peel off the next sheet and butter it, cover with another sheet and set aside. Repeat with two more sheets, so that you have two sheets of double thickness.

Place one doubled sheet lengthways on the table, put the folded square in the centre of it and lay the other doubled sheet on top at 90° to the first sheet, to make a cross-shape that is thickest in the middle.

Carefully lift the pastry cross off the table and place in a 22–24cm ovenproof frying pan or cake tin. Let it line the tin or pan with the sides of the pastry hanging over

the edge. Fill with the chicken mixture and fold the corners over to cover it. We like to make the top a little crumpled so it looks natural. Brush the top of the pastry with the remaining butter and place in the centre of the oven for 15 minutes. After this time, turn the tin around so that the *pastilla* cooks evenly, and bake for a further 10–15 minutes or until the pastry is all golden and crisp.

Serve immediately, with a jug of the warm cooking liquid as sauce and a fresh green salad on the side.

Lamb shawarma

Holly worked with us for a while. We called her 'Holly the friendly ghost' because of her quiet ways and her ability to materialise behind us out of thin air. A staunch vegetarian and lover of small animals, she did not talk to us much, but she did tell us how the smell of this dish made her want to leave her veggie ways for a while. The delicious aroma that is so joyous to diners is the bane of existence for the kitchen staff, especially the girls as the smell gets caught in their hair. They get strange looks on the Tube after work and dogs chasing them on the walk home.

For 6 as a big, fun-filled dinner

4 onions, peeled (about 500g)
3 tbsp ras el hanut spice mix
2 tsp salt
½ tsp white pepper
1 shoulder of lamb, on the bone
   (about 1.8–2kg)

For the cabbage salad
   ½ tsp salt
   ½ white cabbage, shredded (about 350g)
   juice of 1 lemon
   1 small bunch of parsley, chopped
      (about 15–20g)
   2 tbsp vegetable oil
   seeds from 1 small pomegranate
      (if you want)

Preheat your oven to 250°C/230°C fan/ gas mark 9.

Purée the first 2 onions to a pulp in a food processor with the ras el hanut, salt and pepper. Slice the other 2 onions and lay them on the base of a deep roasting dish that is big enough to contain the lamb. Pat the puréed onion mixture all over the lamb, top and bottom, and lay it on the bed of onions.

Place the roasting dish uncovered in the upper-middle part of the very hot oven for 30 minutes. It should have started to colour and brown (it may take another 10 minutes if your oven doesn't run very hot).

Pour in enough water to reach halfway up the lamb joint and cover the dish. Lower the oven temperature to 200°C/180°C fan/ gas mark 6 and cook for 1 hour. Uncover, baste with the liquid at the bottom of the dish, then re-cover and return to the oven. Reduce the heat to 180°C/160°C fan/gas mark 4 and cook for an hour. Baste again, re-cover and cook for a further hour. Basting is important as it will help to soften the lamb, so don't skip doing this. After 3½ hours the meat should be really soft and come away from the bone easily.

Sprinkle the salt on the shredded cabbage in a bowl, mix and allow to sit for 10–15 minutes until it starts to soften. Add the lemon juice, parsley and vegetable oil and mix well. If need be, add a touch more salt – it should be really sharp and lemony. Sprinkle with the pomegranate seeds if using.

Set your table with flatbread to soak up the juices, some yogurt, a bowl of mint leaves to cool, pickled chillies if you want some heat, and some cabbage salad for crunch. Bring the whole beautiful shoulder to the table and dish it out with a large spoon.

Veggie.

Much as we like meat and fish, our go-to comfort foods are always vegetarian – pasta, Israeli couscous, *mujadra* with tahini and salad, or *kusheri* with tomato salsa.

Our *kusheri* has not always been popular with everyone. In Cairo you can buy this dish – rice, lentils, pasta and chickpeas, scented with cumin, caramelised onion and cinnamon – from street vendors, served in a cone of old newspaper and topped with tomato sauce. When we opened the restaurant we had a vision of a bowl on the counter by the window filled with *kusheri*, which we would sell in cones made of old menus. But because we had just opened, we didn't have any old menus yet, so we had to use new paper. And we hadn't thought about how our customers would transport a paper cone filled with rice and tomato sauce back to the office along with their handbags, laptop bags, bicycle bags and any other bags they had. Another hitch was that the office workers of central London, unlike the labourers of Cairo, are quite conscious of their waistlines and tend to avoid carb-explosion dishes of this kind.

We thought we saw a glimmer of hope when a group of Egyptian students from nearby University College London came in, asking whether this was the place that sold *kusheri*... but they came back only to tell us that they thought our version had too much coriander seed in it. After a week of cooking it every morning and feeding it to our staff every night, we decided to drop this dish, much to the delight of the girls, who were tired of cleaning rice from the counter and of eating the same thing for supper every day.

The best thing to come out of this experiment was our friendship with Huda, a lady from Dubai who was going past our restaurant one day and walked in when she saw *kusheri*. She now comes almost every week and has become not only a friend but also a quality controller for our cooking. She warns us when something is not up to scratch and we look for her seal of approval on new dishes, so much do we trust her fine palate. Incidentally, she did not think our *kusheri* recipe was right either, and to show us what it should taste like, she brought us a pot of *kusheri* straight from the kitchens of the Egyptian Embassy, no less, where she has friends.

Our *mujadra* recipe, on the other hand, is knockout. Everyone agrees.

Mujadra with salad & tahini

This is a perfect dinner and needs nothing else, but you could easily add some roasted meat or fish if you wanted to (this works particularly well with lamb chops or kofta).

**Dinner for 4
(or for 2, with
leftovers for lunch
the next day)**

For the lentil rice
2 tbsp olive oil
2–3 onions, peeled, halved and sliced
   (about 400g)
1 tsp + ½ tsp salt
1 litre cold water
150g lentils (we favour Puy, but other
   green ones work well too)
250g Basmati rice (we like Tilda) or
   long-grain Persian rice
½ tsp freshly ground black pepper
a knob of butter (about 25g)

For the salad
3 tomatoes
3 Lebanese cucumbers or 1–1½ regular
   cucumbers
5 sprigs of fresh mint, picked and chopped
5 sprigs of fresh parsley, picked and
   chopped
½ tsp salt
juice of 1–2 lemons
3 tbsp olive oil

240g tahini (page 16)

For the crispy shallots (optional)
vegetable oil, for frying
2–3 long banana shallots, peeled and
   cut into little rings
1 tbsp flour
a pinch of salt, plus more for sprinkling
a pinch of pepper

Put the oil, onions and 1 teaspoon of
salt in a small frying pan and fry for about
15–20 minutes on a gentle heat until the
onions start to go golden. In the meantime
set a saucepan containing the water and
lentils on a high heat and bring to the boil.
Then set a timer for 10 minutes and leave
the lentils to cook – do not turn down
the heat.

Once the onions are caramelised, add the
rice, pepper, butter and the additional

half-teaspoon of salt to the frying pan and
stir to coat the rice all over. Continue frying
for 2–3 minutes, stirring occasionally.
Remove the rice from the heat when it
starts to catch on the base of the pan and
crisp up.

By now the lentils should have had
10 minutes. Tip the rice mixture into the
lentil pan and bring to the boil. Stir once,
then cover, reduce the heat to low and
leave to cook for 10 minutes. Check that
all the water has been absorbed by pushing
the rice aside with a spoon so you can see
the bottom of the pot; if there is still liquid
there, re-cover and cook for an extra
5 minutes. Once the lentils and rice have
absorbed all the water, turn the heat off
and leave to rest covered for 10–15 minutes.

Dice the tomato and cucumber as small
as you can, then combine in a bowl with
the other salad ingredients.

Make the tahini, following the recipe on
page 16.

If you are making crispy shallots, pour a
thick layer of oil into a frying pan and set
over a high heat. Mix the shallot rings,
flour, salt and pepper together in a bowl.
Once the oil is very hot (if you drop in a
pinch of flour, it should fizz up), drop small
batches of shallots into it – they should
start to bubble up straight away. As soon
as each batch has browned, lift it out
with a slotted spoon and drain on kitchen
paper to absorb the excess oil. Once all
the shallots are fried, sprinkle with some
sea salt. They will crisp as they cool.

We like to bring all the various elements of
this dish to the table so that each person
can decide how much rice, salad, tahini
and shallot they want, but you can of
course plate it up individually if you prefer.

Mushroom & cumin sfiha

We call this dish *sfiha* as it is very loosely connected to the traditional Arabic pizza-like dish, in that it consists of a savoury topping (in this case mushroom and cumin) on a rich, yeasted dough. The curd cheese is easy to make yourself (see page 134) but if you can't be bothered, use ricotta instead. If you only cook one dish from this book, make it this one – it's truly wonderful.

Dinner for 4

For the dough
120ml warm water
20g fresh yeast or 1 tbsp dried yeast
1 tsp sugar
190g plain flour
65g wholemeal flour
a pinch of salt
1 egg
50g butter

For the filling
3 onions, peeled and diced (about 450g)
3 cloves of garlic, peeled and thinly sliced
1 small leek, sliced (about 120g)
2 tbsp olive oil
50g butter
1½ tsp salt
1 cinnamon stick
500g mushrooms, thickly sliced (I like to mix chestnut and button)
2 tbsp ground cumin
1 tsp freshly ground black pepper

For the cheesy layer
200g curd cheese (page 134) or ricotta
1 egg
½ tsp freshly ground black pepper

Start with the filling: sauté the onions, garlic and leek with the oil, butter, salt and cinnamon stick on a medium heat so the vegetables soften rather than colour – this will take about 10–15 minutes. Once they start to stick to the bottom of the pan, it is time to add the sliced mushrooms. They will start to let out water and after about 15–20 minutes their volume should have halved. Add the cumin and black pepper and continue cooking till there is no liquid left in the pan. Taste and adjust the seasoning if necessary, then leave to cool.

Mix the water, yeast and sugar together in a cup, stir and set aside for 10–15 minutes to bubble up. Put the flours, salt, egg and butter in a large bowl and pour the foaming yeast on top. Mix to combine and work to a smoothish dough (the wholemeal flour will give a slightly rough texture). Form into a ball and cover the bowl with cling film. Set aside to prove in a warm place until doubled in size.

Mix the curd with the egg and pepper in a small bowl until well combined.

Preheat your oven to 220°C/200°C fan/gas mark 7. Line a 22–24cm ovenproof frying pan (or baking tin) with a piece of grease-proof paper so that it overhangs the sides a little. Remove the greaseproof paper from the pan and place on your work surface.

Spread the dough on the paper – pat it and push it into place so the sides of the dough come all the way up the edges of the paper. Lift the dough and paper up together and lay them in the frying pan with the edges overhanging the sides.

Fill the base of the pan with the curd mix and smooth it around. Top with the mushroom filling. Fold the overhanging sides of the dough back down onto the filling. Leave in a warm place to prove for 20–30 minutes.

Bake in the centre of the oven for 15 minutes, then reduce the heat to 180°C/160°C fan/gas mark 4 and bake for another 10 minutes. Serve hot from the oven or at room temperature, with a nice salad to accompany it. Do not offer your guests seconds – squirrel away any that is left over for the next day; it'll still be delicious.

Medias – courgettes filled with lemon rice & currants

We were concerned about Eve: she started showing up to work with black marks all over her body. We thought she might be in an abusive relationship. Turns out it wasn't abusive, just very passionate. In the high-school spirit that governs Honey & Co, we started taking bets on where the next bite mark would turn up, and we named the boyfriend 'The octopus-vampire'. We imagined him to be a bloodthirsty monster. Eve would not bring him over to meet us, knowing we would embarrass her. I ran into them on the Tube to Brixton one day, and Eve was duly embarrassed. The octo-vamp turned out to be a well-mannered, skinny PhD student, and a vegetarian as well. We were no longer concerned.

**Serves 4
as a main**

4 even-sized courgettes
2 tbsp olive oil
1 onion, peeled and finely diced (about 120g)
½ cinnamon stick
½ tsp + ½ tsp salt
½ tsp ground turmeric
½ tsp ground pimento (allspice)
a pinch of cayenne pepper, plus another
  pinch to garnish
125g risotto rice
40g dried currants
2 tbsp lemon juice (juice of 1 lemon)
375ml water
4–5 cherry tomatoes (about 75g)
1 small bunch of parsley (about 15–20g),
  picked and chopped – reserve a little
  for garnish
1 tbsp chopped dill (3–4 sprigs)

Halve the courgettes lengthways. Use a teaspoon to remove the seeds and create little boats. Lay them in a baking tray with sides that come up higher than the courgettes. It should look like a little marina with all the boats lined up.

Preheat your oven to 200°C/180°C fan/gas mark 6.

Heat the oil in a frying pan over a medium heat. It may seem like a lot, but it is the only fat going into the entire dish, and it adds lots of flavour. Fry the onion, cinnamon stick and half a teaspoon of salt gently in the oil so that the onion softens, rather than colours. Then add the turmeric, pimento and cayenne and mix really well. Cook for 30 seconds, then tip in the risotto rice and stir to coat. Add the other half-teaspoon of salt and the currants, and pour over the lemon juice and water. Bring to the boil. Allow to boil for 1 minute, then drain through a colander sitting over a bowl. Retain the cooking liquid.

Cut the cherry tomatoes into thin slices. Stir into the rice along with the chopped parsley and dill, and mix well. Divide the rice mixture between the courgette boats. Bear in mind that the rice will expand as it cooks, so don't overfill them. Pour the cooking liquid into the tray so the courgettes are about half-submerged; if you need to, add a little water to top up.

Place a sheet of greaseproof paper directly on top of the courgettes and cover the baking tin with aluminium foil so that it is entirely sealed. This enables the courgettes to steam in the cooking liquid.

Cook in the centre of the oven for 30 minutes, then carefully remove, baste the courgettes with the liquid at the base of the tin and cover again. Return to the oven for another 30 minutes, after which they should be ready to serve. You can check by inserting a small knife into the side of a courgette – it should be very soft.

Baste the courgettes again so they are nice and juicy, and sprinkle with the reserved parsley and additional pinch of cayenne. We like to serve this with some fresh goats' yogurt and a green salad.

Israeli couscous, peas, preserved lemon, mint & goats' cheese

This is a great one for midweek as it takes no more than 20 minutes from slicing the leeks to serving the finished dish, but it is good enough for weekends as well – filling, fresh and very tasty. And you really don't want to spend the weekend stuck in the kitchen...

Israeli couscous comes in lots of different shapes – little spheres, hoops, stars or rice grains, like the ones in the picture. They all work. You can use Palestinian *maftoul*, Greek or Italian *orzo*, or *fregola* from Sardinia instead, but these may need more water and a longer cooking time. *Mougrabiah* will not work here.

Serves 2 as a main, or 4 as a side dish

2 tbsp olive oil
1 small leek, sliced and washed (about 120g)
4 cloves of garlic, peeled and sliced
2 tsp salt
1 preserved lemon (page 14), diced (about 2 tbsp)
250g Israeli couscous (also called giant couscous or ptitim)
700ml boiling water
200g shelled fresh peas
4 sprigs of mint, picked and chopped
4 sprigs of parsley, picked and chopped
100g goats' cheese of your choice

Heat the oil in a large sauté pan or non-stick wok. Fry the leeks and garlic on a medium heat for 2–3 minutes to soften, then add the salt and preserved lemon, and stir to combine. Tip in the Israeli couscous and continue frying for another 2 minutes or until the little couscous balls start to go golden.

Add half the boiling water and the peas. Boil until most of the water has soaked in, then add the rest of the water and cook on a high heat until it has also been sucked up by the couscous.

Remove from the heat, add the mint and parsley and stir well. Finally crumble the goats' cheese all over and serve.

Butternut stew with dumplings

This is a journey that took a strange twist. I remembered having 'fake *kubbe*' at a friend's house – spicy, light-textured dumplings served in soup; dumplings which looked like *kubbe* but had no meat filling. We experimented a lot, trying to recreate them and failing time and again, then we decided to revert to making Ashkenazi *kneidl*. They worked a treat. Try cooking these dumplings with the beetroot broth on page 168 for a variation on traditional beetroot *kubbe* soup.

Dinner for 4, with maybe some left over

For the soup
2 tbsp olive oil
1–2 onions, peeled and diced (about 250g)
4 cloves of garlic, peeled and halved
    lengthways
1 tsp + 1 tsp salt
1 butternut squash, peeled, deseeded and
    diced in large cubes (about 600g)
2 small carrots, peeled and sliced
3 celery sticks, sliced
2 whole dried Persian lemons, cut in half
    (try and get these as they add
    a great flavour)
½ cinnamon stick
1 tbsp whole fennel seeds
1 tbsp whole coriander seeds
2–3 ripe tomatoes, diced (about 250g)
1 tsp ground turmeric
1 tsp smoky paprika
a pinch of cayenne pepper
2 litres water

For the dumplings
2 eggs
½ tsp salt
½ tsp ground coriander
¼ tsp freshly ground black pepper
¼ tsp ground cinnamon
2 tbsp vegetable oil
95g matzo meal
60ml sparkling water (for a fluffier texture;
    but still water also works)

Heat the oil in a frying pan over a medium heat. Add the onions, garlic and 1 teaspoon of salt. Sauté until the onions and garlic soften, then stir in the butternut, carrots and celery. Continue cooking till the vegetables start to catch on the bottom of the pan – this will take about 5–10 minutes. Add the Persian lemons, cinnamon stick, fennel seeds, coriander seeds and the rest of the salt. Sauté together for 2 minutes, then add the tomatoes and ground spices. Allow to cook for 5 minutes before pouring in the water and bringing the mixture to the boil. Once it has boiled, skim and reduce the heat to a simmer. Partially cover the pan and leave to simmer for 40–50 minutes until all the vegetables are very soft.

While the soup is simmering, whisk the eggs to a fluffy mass with the salt, spices and oil. Slowly whisk in the matzo meal. Finally, whisk in the water. Cover and leave to rest in the fridge for at least half an hour, until your soup is ready.

Use damp hands to form the matzo mixture into sixteen small balls and pop them into the soup. Increase the heat and return the soup to the boil, then reduce back to a simmer. Cover and simmer for 30 minutes until the dumplings have fluffed up, then serve in wide flat bowls. Allow three or four dumplings per person.

Cauliflower 'shawarma'

This obviously isn't really a shawarma – there is no lamb and no fat – but it is a way of slow-cooking cauliflower that makes it feel substantial and tasty enough to warrant the association. When we have this on the menu in the restaurant, we use deep-fried purple cauliflower and boiled Italian Romesco cauliflower (the green one that looks like an alien), cooked in salt water, in addition to slow-roasted white cauliflower. The purple and green ones taste like regular cauliflower but add colour and texture. They are not central to the success of the dish, but if you see either type in a farmers' market and can't resist buying them, this is not a bad way to use them.

**Serves 2
as a main**

1 medium-sized cauliflower, leaves
   still attached
2 tbsp olive oil
3 tbsp baharat spice mix (page 12)
1 tsp sea salt

For the caramelised onions
   2 large onions, peeled and sliced
      (about 300g)
   1 tbsp olive oil
   ½ tsp salt
   1 tsp sugar

For the tahini dressing
   1 lemon
   125g tahini paste
   a pinch of salt
   100–130ml water

For the garnish
   2 tbsp roasted pine nuts
   1 tsp sumac (not essential)
   lavoush crackers (page 64) or crispy
      pitta shards (page 124)

Preheat your oven to 200°C/180°C fan/ gas mark 6.

Place the whole cauliflower, leaves and all, in an ovenproof saucepan that fits it snugly. Fill the bottom of the pan with enough water to just cover the stem and leaves. Drizzle the oil all over the florets and sprinkle with the spice mix and sea salt – it will look like a lot, but you want a layer of spice as a crust. Place in the oven and roast for 1–1½ hours. You will know it is cooked when you can insert a small knife through the centre of the cauliflower all the way down into the stem and it goes in easily.

While the cauliflower is cooking, place the sliced onions in a frying pan with the oil and salt and fry on a low heat until they start to soften and go golden. Add the sugar and continue cooking until the onions are caramelised and brown. Remove from the heat.

Halve the lemon. Mix the tahini paste in a small bowl with the juice from one half of the lemon and the salt. Add 100ml of water and mix well. Continue mixing and adding water very slowly until the paste loosens to a creamy texture.

Carefully lift the cooked cauliflower out of the water and cut it into thick slices, including the stem and the leaves, which will taste great after the slow-cooking. Divide the cauliflower between two plates. Squeeze the juice from the remaining half of the lemon all over, then top with the caramelised onions and tahini paste. Garnish with the pine nuts and the sumac (if using) and serve with the crispy flat bread.

Aubergines

We take great pride in our produce. Sinan, our monosyllabic fruit and veg guy, tends to arrive 2 hours late and with only some of what we ordered, but he knows how to choose the best watermelons (a dying art) and we can count on him for the small, crunchy cucumbers we love, exactly the kind of green chillies we need, and black Bursa figs in season. Sabrina brings us the best of Europe – crazy coloured cauliflowers from France; garlic flowers from Cornwall for ten days in July; sweet tomatoes and round aubergines from southern Italy. These aubergines have a sweet, white flesh without a hint of bitterness and are a particular joy to cook and eat – if you ever see them in the shops, treat yourself. That said, most supermarkets stock terrific aubergines these days, so if you can't find them, don't feel as if you are missing out.

The aubergine has somehow become a meat substitute and features heavily in vegetarian menus. It seems that if you're a vegetarian and don't like aubergines, you are doomed to starvation or salad. These are three of our favourite aubergine recipes – they're the ones we always go back to in our menus and are favoured by meat-eaters and vegetarians alike.

Vegetarian moussaka

This dish was inspired by Nirit Putterman, a food-fanatic and friend who sends us long emails about venison stew and has been known to call us in the middle of the night with questions about the water-fat ratio in choux pastry, and again in the morning to report the results of her baking. Like all her dishes, this has been meticulously tried and tested, and rightly judged to be delicious.

A hearty dinner for 4

4 large aubergines, trimmed
olive oil, for brushing and drizzling
sea salt
freshly ground black pepper
100g goats' cheese (we prefer a log, but you
    can use a soft one if you prefer)
25g kashkaval (or pecorino) cheese, grated

For the tomato sauce
    1 large red onion, peeled and diced
        (about 150g)
    6 cloves of garlic, peeled and crushed
    ½ cinnamon stick
    2 thick slices of lemon
    4 sprigs of fresh oregano, picked
    2 tbsp olive oil
    1 tsp salt
    6–8 large plum tomatoes, diced
        (about 700g)
    1 tsp sugar
    1 tbsp tomato purée
    ½ tsp freshly ground black pepper
    2 tbsp water

Preheat the oven to 220°C/200°C fan/ gas mark 7.

Slice each aubergine into four or five slices lengthways. Brush a baking tray with olive oil and place the slices flat on it. Drizzle with some more oil and season with sea salt and black pepper. Roast in the oven for 12 minutes, then turn the tray around to ensure that the slices cook evenly. Roast for another 8–12 minutes until they go golden and soft. Set aside to cool.

Sauté the onion, garlic, cinnamon stick, lemon slices and oregano with the oil and salt in a frying pan over a medium heat, until the onion and garlic start to soften.

Add half the diced tomatoes and the sugar. Increase the heat to high and cook for about 8–10 minutes, stirring occasionally, until the tomatoes go very soft. Add the remaining tomato dice along with the tomato purée, black pepper and water and continue cooking over a high heat for another 6–8 minutes. Remove the cinnamon stick, but you can leave the lemon slices in the pan – they taste really good.

Cover the base of a small casserole dish or ovenproof saucepan (about 20cm diameter) with a layer of the cooked aubergines and spoon a third of the tomato sauce on top. Smooth it out a little and crumble half the goats' cheese all over. Repeat the process with a second layer of aubergine slices, another third of the tomato sauce and the rest of the goats' cheese. Cover with the remaining aubergines and sauce, and sprinkle with the grated kashkaval. You can prepare up to this stage a day in advance – just cover and store in the fridge until needed. Then 30 minutes before you want to serve, take the moussaka out of the fridge to come to room temperature and preheat the oven to 200°C/180°C fan/ gas mark 6.

Bake in the centre of the oven for 20–25 minutes, or until the kashkaval cheese topping is all melted and golden.

Badargani – aubergine rolls filled with walnuts & pomegranate

This is a festive, colourful, good-looking vegetarian dish with tons of flavour. You can serve this as a starter if you want, or as a main with some yogurt and a large green salad.

Dinner for 4

4 large aubergines, trimmed
olive oil, for brushing and drizzling
sea salt
freshly ground black pepper

For the filling
   1 large red onion (about 150g)
   3 tbsp olive oil
   ½ tsp salt
   100g toasted walnuts, roughly chopped
      (reserve 2 tbsp to garnish)
   2 tbsp pomegranate molasses
   ½ tsp freshly ground black pepper
   5cm piece of fresh ginger, peeled and grated
   1 small bunch of parsley, chopped
      (about 15–20g)
   100g fresh pomegranate seeds
      (reserve 2 tbsp to garnish)
   a pinch of cayenne

Heat the oven to 220°C/200°C fan/gas mark 7.

Slice each aubergine into five or six slices lengthways. Keep the outside slices for the filling and use the nice, long, inside slices for the rolls. Brush a baking tray with oil and place the nice inside slices flat on it. Drizzle with some more oil and season with sea salt and black pepper. Roast in the oven for 12 minutes, then turn the tray around to ensure that the slices cook evenly. Roast for another 8–12 minutes until they are golden and soft. Set aside to cool.

While the slices are in the oven, peel the onion and dice finely. Cut the aubergine trimmings (the outside slices) into the same sized cubes. Fry the onion in the oil over a medium heat until it starts to soften, then add the diced aubergine and the salt. Cook until the aubergine goes very soft. Remove the pan from the stove and add the remaining ingredients. Mix well and taste to see if you would like to adjust the seasoning.

Place a large spoonful of the filling at one end of each roasted aubergine slice and roll them into thick sausages. Place the filled aubergine rolls in an ovenproof serving dish. If you have a little filling left over, spread it around the edges of the dish. Place in the oven for 5 minutes to warm through before serving. Sprinkle the warmed rolls with the reserved walnuts and pomegranate seeds and serve 3 rolls per person.

Aubergine sabich

There is much debate about the origins of this dish, but I don't find that important or interesting. What no one debates is what a good combo this is – rich fried egg and rich tahini, sharp lemon and fresh parsley, and bread to soak it all up. There is nothing sophisticated here, nothing refined, just pure and shameless greed. Tuck in...

A light meal for 2 – breakfast, lunch or dinner

1 large aubergine, trimmed (about 300g)
olive oil, for brushing, drizzling and frying
sea salt
freshly ground black pepper
2 pitta (page 56)
2–4 eggs
120g tahini (page 16)

For the chilli-garlic dressing
  ½ small red chilli
  ½ small green chilli
  3 cloves of garlic, peeled
  ¼ tsp cumin
  ¼ tsp salt
  1 tsp honey
  juice of 1 lemon
  1 small bunch of parsley (about 15–20g), picked and chopped
  2 tbsp olive oil

Deseed the chillies and cut into the smallest dice you can manage. Cut the garlic as small as you can too. Mix the chillies and garlic with all the other dressing ingredients in a small bowl and set aside while you prepare the rest of the dish.

Preheat your oven to 240°C/220°C fan/gas mark 9.

Slice the aubergine thickly – about the width of your thumb. Brush a roasting tin with olive oil and lay the aubergine slices flat on the base of it, with no overlaps. Drizzle some more olive oil over the top (be generous, it adds loads of flavour) and sprinkle with sea salt and black pepper. Place in the top of the oven to roast for 18–20 minutes until the slices are golden. Remove the aubergine from the oven.

Put the pitta in the oven for 2–3 minutes until it is very warm. Fry the eggs (1–2 per person) in a little olive oil in a frying pan – I cook them over a medium-low heat as I like to set the whites entirely. While they are frying, split the pitta and place, opened-up, on individual plates. Divide the aubergine slices between the two open pitta and dress generously with the chilli dressing. Spoon the tahini all over and place the perfectly-fried eggs on top. Eat now.

Savoury cheesecake

This is a base preparation from which you can derive dozens of different versions. It really is a cheesecake, and flourless as well (though you can sprinkle it with some crunchy breadcrumbs if you want), but unlike sweet cheesecake, it is only truly delicious when eaten warm and oven-fresh – it does not cool down well.

For 3–4 as a main, served with a side salad

For the basic cheesecake
200g full fat cream cheese (we use Philadelphia)
200g feta, crumbled
100g soft goats' cheese, crumbled
½ tsp freshly ground black pepper
3 eggs

Preheat your oven to 190°C/170°C fan/ gas mark 5.

Mix all the cheesecake ingredients together in a food processor to combine thoroughly and then transfer to a lightly-buttered baking dish (a 20cm-diameter casserole dish is best).

Use any one of the following vegetable preparations, or try your own combination (any vegetable you like can work, but if you want to use something with high water content such as spinach or tomatoes, it is best to cook or roast it first). Just half-submerge the vegetables in the cheesecake mix and put the dish in the oven to bake. Set a timer for 15 minutes, then turn the dish around (so that it cooks evenly) and allow another 10 minutes, by which time the cheesecake should just be going golden. Bring it to table in the dish it was cooked in, along with a big spoon to dish it up.

Aubergine
Use 2 aubergines. Cut each one into eight wedges and place in a roasting tray. Brush with olive oil (about 2–3 tablespoons), season with sea salt and a hint of pepper, and roast in a hot oven (220°C/200°C fan/ gas mark 7) for 20 minutes or until golden.

Roasted courgettes and mint
Use 3–4 courgettes. Cut into disks (about as thick as a finger) and place on a roasting tray. Brush with a little olive oil (about 1 tablespoon) and season with sea salt and pepper. Roast at 220°C/200°C fan/gas mark 7 for 20 minutes. Mix with about 15 whole mint leaves while the courgette slices are cooling.

Roasted peppers, Kalamata olives and oregano
Use 3 red or yellow peppers. Follow the roasting instructions as for canned peppers on page 43 up to the point where you tear them into strips, then mix with the picked leaves from 3–4 sprigs of fresh oregano (or basil, if you prefer) and a handful of pitted olives.

Dessert.

When we saw 25a Warren Street for the first time, it was the large front window that got us most. It faces the mainly pedestrian street, along which commuters from Great Portland Street station walk to UCLH and back, and commuters from Warren Street station walk to their offices in inner Fitzrovia and back, all avoiding the ugly Euston Road in favour of quaint little Warren Street during the morning and evening rush hours. Twice a day the street is filled with people, and people like cake.

As we could not afford to pay for PR, we decided to bake some, and so our cakes became our advertisement and our bait. Glistening with syrup and glowing with fruit, we laid them on the window counter to whore themselves to the street. People would double-take at our window during their daily dash, then pause and come back for a closer look at our lovelies – the cherry-topped one, the spicy brown one, the half-glazed-half-naked one. Then Itamar or Rachael would meet them at the door, show them a menu, have a chat, bring them in… The cakes were doing their job.

We met some of our best friends and customers in this way. People like the beautiful Pilar, who is an expert on the chocolate hazelnut loaf. And like our Fitzroy Square neighbours Fay and Reg, a very stylish couple who walked by in pressed linen one summer's evening, stopped at our window and were shame-lessly accosted by Itamar, but returned in spite of it, and hopefully will continue to do so for a long time to come.

As we got busier, the cakes had to vacate their window seat for paying customers and now spend most of the day on the back bar instead. I was happy. True, serving cake as pudding wasn't what I had planned to do when we opened, and I don't think that cake is always the best dessert to finish with, but I was too busy to think of adding anything else to the menu. Then a group of chefs who had worked with me at my last job came to eat at the restaurant, to see what I was up to. It was great fun to see them, particularly to see them in my role as a friend and not as their chef. I sent them the entire menu and waited to see what they said. My boy Marky Sparky was the only one to be absolutely honest – about everything, but the thing that got me the most was when he said, 'Mama, you should do plated desserts from the kitchen. I don't get it. Desserts are your thing. Why are you just baking cakes?' I shrugged at him and said that with all the baked goods, the jams, the cakes and the rest of the food, there was no way I had time to make anything more. But in truth, he was right. Dessert is where my heart is, and what our menu needed, and I was just avoiding it to make life easier. The next week I set the feta and honey cheesecake in front of Itamar.

Now, the reason I love making desserts is that I love watching people while they eat them: they become quieter for a while, then happier, and then they feel they can really relax. I love making desserts for Itamar in particular. He will wake up in the morning and say, 'I dreamed of marzipan – a cake soft and oozing with little chunks of marzipan that melt in your mouth,' and off I trot to produce his dreams. There is a saying that the way to a person's heart is through their stomach. Well, if you see pictures of slim Itamar before we met, you will realise that I have most likely been the reason for his considerable growth since then…

The recipes in this chapter are a great way to win over a loved one, to celebrate an evening, to enjoy good company and most of all to indulge yourself and the people around you.

Basic pastry instructions

- **It is best to use scales when making** pastry and to buy a set of measuring spoons for maximum accuracy. Follow the measurements as closely as you can.

- **The starting temperature of your** ingredients will greatly affect the end result. It is best to use room-temperature butter, flour and eggs unless otherwise stated.

- **I use unsalted butter for all my recipes.**

- **I always preheat my oven to give it** time to reach the required temperature, and I always bake in the centre of the oven unless the recipe says otherwise.

- **I do most of my baking (sweet and** savoury) in a fan-assisted oven, as it is faster and gives better heat distribution than a convection oven. I have given settings for convection and gas ovens too, but you will need to use an element of discretion with regard to baking times as every oven cooks differently.

Dessert.

Feta & honey cheesecake on a kadaif pastry base

This dessert tends to get plenty of compliments and has become our signature dish. It is quite complex, with a few different components, and is quite ambitious for home preparation – not because the stages are difficult, but because there are a few of them. However, there was no way I could write this book without putting the recipe in it. You can use a generic supermarket feta, but for a finish that is smooth and salty, buy one of the tinned smooth fetas sold in Middle Eastern delis. It will be worth it. *Kadaif* is the strangest, most amazing pastry; it is made out of tiny thin noodles that you bake with butter and sugar. The best thing to do is to buy it ready-made in a Middle Eastern grocery store; use what you need for this recipe and keep the rest in the freezer for next time. However, if you can't find *kadaif*, use filo pastry and shred it as finely as you can with a knife or a pair of scissors. The advantage of this dish is that each part can be made in advance and assembled just before you are going to eat – just as we do at Honey & Co. So it is good for stress-free entertaining (although not so much for stress-free preparation). You could simply make the cheesecake cream and place it in a large bowl, sprinkling with some nuts and drizzling with honey; not quite the same, but still tasty.

Makes a generous 4 portions

For the kadaif base
25g melted butter
50g kadaif *pastry (or shredded filo)*
1 tbsp caster sugar

For the cheesecake cream
160g full fat cream cheese
  (we use Philadelphia)
160ml extra thick double cream
40g icing sugar
40g honey of your choice (a grainy one
  works best, in my opinion)
50g smooth, creamy feta
seeds from ½ vanilla pod (or 1 tsp
  vanilla essence)

For the honey syrup
50ml honey
50ml water

For the garnish
a few fresh oregano or marjoram leaves
a handful of whole roasted almonds,
  roughly chopped
some mellow-flavoured seasonal fruit
  – white peaches or blueberries are best
  (although raspberries or apricots are
  also good)

Preheat the oven to 180°C/160°C fan/ gas mark 4.

Mix the melted butter with the pastry and sugar in a bowl. Fluff the pastry by pulling it and loosening the shreds with your hands till it gets an even coating of sugar and butter. Divide into four equal amounts, pulling each clump of pastry out of the mass like a little ball of yarn. Place these on a baking tray lined with parchment paper. They should resemble four flat birds' nests, each about the size of a drinks coaster.

Bake for about 12–15 minutes or until golden. Allow to cool and keep in an airtight container until ready to serve. The pastry nests will keep for 2–3 days, so you can prepare them well in advance. »»

Place all the cheesecake cream ingredients in a large bowl and combine with a spatula or a big spoon, using circular folding motions until the mixture thickens and starts to hold the swirls. Don't use a whisk: it's vital not to add air to the mixture as the secret is in the texture. Check that it is sufficiently thick by scooping some onto a spoon and turning it upside-down: it should stay where it is. If it is still too soft, mix it some more. (If you are increasing the quantities in this recipe to feed lots of people, I suggest using a paddle on a mixer for this, but you'll need to watch it like a hawk so it doesn't turn into butter.) You can prepare the cheesecake cream in advance (up to 48 hours before serving) and keep it covered in the fridge until it is time to assemble the dessert.

Put the honey and water for the syrup in a small pan and boil together for 1 minute, skimming off any foam or impurities that come to the top. Remove from the hob and leave to cool, then store covered in the fridge until you are ready to serve.

When you come to assemble the dessert, place a pastry nest on each plate and top with a generous scoop of the cheesecake mix. Sprinkle over the herb leaves and chopped nuts, add a few blueberries or a couple of slices of peach, and drizzle a tablespoon of the honey syrup over everything. If you want to be super-luxurious, drizzle with some raw honey as well.

Chestnut cake with salted caramel sauce

Our first Christmas was just around the corner. Itamar and I were talking about desserts. 'Do you remember the chestnut cake we used to make at the OXO Tower Restaurant?' Giorgia, at the pastry, dropped the whisk she was holding and turned to us, drooling. By the time we were discussing the salted caramel sauce that went with the cake, she had nearly turned into a puddle. This is one of our most successful desserts and has gained us many compliments, not only from Giorgia; the fact that it is flourless is an added bonus. Many people find making caramel scary: they should, as it can be dangerous. Make sure to use a cloth and do not use your fingers for wiping or tasting. The first time I made a successful crème caramel as a teenager I very carefully poured the caramel into little ramekins and filled the empty pan with cold water. I felt so proud of myself until I decided to check whether the caramel had set by sticking my finger into it. It did set – on my fingertip, and was very painful to remove, so do wait before attempting to taste, touch or try it.

Makes a 24cm diameter cake, enough for 8 generous portions (you can halve the quantities and use an 18cm-diameter tin if you prefer – the baking time will be the same)

For the cake
250g cooked chestnuts
200ml milk
50ml whisky
4 eggs, separated
50g ground almonds
125g sugar

For the salted caramel sauce
75g sugar
1 tbsp honey
30ml water
50ml double cream

Break up the cooked chestnuts a little, place in a saucepan, cover with the milk and set on a low heat to bring them slowly up to the boil. Watch that the milk doesn't boil over. Cook slowly for 15–20 minutes until the chestnuts are really soft – check by pressing one to the side of the saucepan with a spoon; it should crush easily. Remove from the heat and allow to cool for 20–30 minutes until just warm.

Preheat your oven to 180°C/160°C fan/gas mark 4 and line a 24cm-diameter cake tin with baking parchment.

Blitz the chestnuts and milk with a stick blender or in a food processor until they form a smooth, thick paste. Add the whisky and blitz again. Fold in the egg yolks one at a time, then the ground almonds.

Use an electric whisk or a mixer with a whisk attachment to whip the egg whites with the sugar until they are light and fluffy, and form a silky meringue. Take a large spoon of the meringue and stir it into the chestnut paste to loosen it. Then fold the rest of the egg whites in carefully, trying to keep as much air as possible.

Pour into the tin and smooth the top. Place in the centre of the oven and bake for 15 minutes, then turn the cake around so that it cooks evenly and bake for a further 10 minutes. It should be set to a light touch and your finger should come away dry. Allow to cool a little in the tin before taking out of the tin to cool completely. You can keep it covered in the fridge for a couple of days until you are ready to serve.

Mix the sugar, honey and water in a saucepan, making sure the sides of the pan stay clean. The best way to do this is to start by putting the honey in, then the sugar, then pour the water slowly in a circle down the sides of the pan. This should stop any little sugar crystals forming on the sides and ruining your caramel. Set on a high heat and bring to a rapid boil. Don't stir it at all – if you feel the need, rotate the pan in a circular motion to mix a little.

While the sugar solution is boiling, warm the cream for 15–30 seconds in the microwave, or for a couple of minutes in a small pan over a low heat. It is best not to add cold cream to hot caramel as it will seize immediately.

When the sugar solution starts to change colour and become golden, remove the pan from the heat and stir in the warm cream really slowly – use a long wooden spoon and stand away from the pan. Return to the heat to make sure all the sugar has dissolved and combined, then add a pinch of sea salt and remove from the heat again. Allow the sauce to cool before you try it – caramel is no laughing matter, as it gets really hot. Transfer to a pouring jug or other container. The empty pan will clean easily if you fill it with warm water and allow it to rest for a while.

You can make the sauce up to a week in advance and keep it in a covered container in the fridge. You may need to warm it slightly before serving, and you can do that in the microwave or on the stove.

I think this cake is best served warm, so pop each slice in the microwave for 30 seconds to heat up a little, particularly if you have been storing it in the fridge. Then just pour the caramel over and, if you want, serve with some sour cream on the side. If you don't own a microwave, serve the cake at room temperature and heat the caramel on the stove before pouring it over the individual slices to warm them up.

Marzipan & almond cakes with roasted plums

A certain percentage of the population are 'marzipan fiends'. They look at our dessert menu, see this and light up, their choice made in seconds (or years ago, actually). I'd like to say my husband is one such fiend, as he loves marzipan, but he is just as keen on chocolate, caramel, creamy things, fruity things, any dessert really...

This makes 6 small individual cakes (I use baby loaf tins but round muffin tins will do the trick). You can double the recipe to make a 24cm diameter cake, enough for 10–12 people; just increase the baking time to 25–30 minutes

For the cakes
100g butter
50g caster sugar
60g dark brown sugar
2 eggs
30g wholemeal flour
a pinch of salt
80g ground almonds
25g whole almonds, roughly chopped
*   (I prefer them with the skin on)*
50g marzipan, broken into little chunks

For the roasted plums
4–6 plums (depending on size; I allow
*   ½–1 per person)*
½ vanilla pod (or substitute 2 star anise,
*   for a different flavour)*
100g caster sugar

Prepare six small individual tins or silicone moulds – spray with butter spray or brush with melted butter. Preheat your oven to 180°C/160°C fan/gas mark 4.

Cream the butter and two sugars together in a mixer, or with a wide spoon in a bowl, until they are well combined and the butter starts to aerate. Don't overwork the mixture until it is too fluffy, as this will make the texture too light and it will resemble a sponge; you are looking to create a heavy, sticky cake with a dense texture. Mix in the eggs one at a time, then add the flour, salt and ground almonds and combine well. Fold in the chopped almonds and marzipan chunks. Divide the batter between the baking tins.

Bake for 12–16 minutes until lightly golden all over the top. Don't be tempted to leave the cakes in a little longer – they need to be gooey inside and the marzipan should stay soft and ooze. They may look a little pale, but the flavour will compensate for that. You can serve these straight away, but if you are preparing them in advance, allow to cool in the moulds, then simply pop them out and store, covered, in the fridge.

Increase the oven temperature to 220°C/200°C fan/gas mark 7.

Quarter the plums (or, if they are large, cut into six) and place in a baking tin or an ovenproof frying pan that fits them snugly. Scrape the seeds out of the half vanilla pod and mix with the sugar. Place the empty pod on the plums and sprinkle the sugar all over. If you decide to use star anise instead of vanilla, just place them with the plums. (If you can only find vanilla sugar rather than whole vanilla pods, use 50:50 vanilla sugar and caster.)

Place the baking tin on the top shelf of the oven and roast for 8–10 minutes. The cooking time really depends on how soft the plums are to start with; you want liquid to begin oozing out of them, so if they need a little longer, return them to the oven. Once the juices have started to run out, shake the tin well so that the plums are coated in the liquid and all the sugar is melted. Allow to cool down.

You can prepare the cakes and plums up to 2–3 days in advance and store them in the fridge until you are ready to serve. You can warm them a little in a microwave (20 seconds each) before serving with the plums and a large dollop of sour cream. Personally I love the contrast of cold plums spooned over warm cake, but you could do it the other way round and keep the cake at room temperature and warm the plums instead.

Saffron & lemon syrup cake

This is a good one for the dead of winter. The lemon rounds glow in saffron like little suns, lighting up your palate with their bright flavour.

This makes a 24cm diameter round cake because I think it looks amazing as a large cake, but if you only want to make a few portions, halve the recipe (and the baking time) and bake in 6 muffin tins

200g butter
270g sugar
4 eggs
200g ground almonds
a pinch of turmeric
140g semolina
2 tbsp plain flour
1 lemon, juice and zest
a pinch of salt
½ tsp baking powder

For the syrup and topping
  2 lemons, really thinly sliced
  enough water to cover x 2, plus 400ml
  250g sugar
  a pinch of turmeric
  a pinch of saffron

Preheat the oven to 180°C/160°C fan/ gas mark 4. Grease a 24 cm diameter cake tin with greaseproof paper.

Place the lemon slices for the syrup and topping in a small saucepan, cover with water and bring to the boil over a high heat. Drain the slices, re-cover with water and bring to the boil again. Drain for a second time (by now all the bitterness should be gone), then cover with 400ml of fresh water. Add the sugar, turmeric and saffron and bring to the boil, reduce the heat to low and simmer for 6–8 minutes until the peel is soft and the syrup has thickened. Remove from the heat.

Use a fork to lift the slices of lemon out of the syrup and layer them, just slightly overlapping, all over the base and a little way up the sides of the lined baking tin; the sugar will help them to stick in place. You may not need all of the lemon slices. Pour over 2 tablespoons of the syrup and reserve the rest for later.

Cream the butter and sugar together in a mixer, or with a wide spoon in a bowl, until they are well combined but not fluffy, as you do not want to aerate the mixture. Stir in the eggs, ground almonds and turmeric, then fold in the semolina, flour, lemon juice and zest, salt and baking powder. Mix well and pour into the cake tin. Bake in the centre of the oven for 15–20 minutes, then turn the cake around to ensure that it bakes evenly and bake for a further 10–15 minutes. The cake should be golden and firm. Remove from the oven and pour over all the remaining syrup to soak in. Allow to rest for 20 minutes before turning out.

The cake needs to be turned on its head to serve, so place a plate on top of the tin and flip it over so the bottom-side is uppermost. Gently remove the tin and the paper. Now, turn off the lights and watch it glow.

Honey parfait

It was Rob's birthday. He and Michelle hosted a party at the restaurant. I rolled up 25 small cones of brown parchment, placed them pointy-end down in empty egg cartons, filled them with honey parfait and put a stick in each one so people could eat them like an ice cream on a stick. Later that summer night the noisy dining room went completely quiet as we handed these out. The sight of 25 lawyers licking these parfaits and grinning like kids was truly magical. Though this is a very simple dessert, the flavours are sophisticated and elegant; the honey flavour comes through powerfully and the cream is, as always, a great partner to it. You can use the simple ice cream moulds that get sold everywhere in summertime to make kids' ice creams or, if you are feeling ambitious, get rolling greaseproof paper and place each cone in a cup in the freezer while it sets. It is hard to give you an exact yield for this recipe, as it will depend on the size of mould you use, but it should make a minimum of 4 popsicles. Any left over can stay in the freezer and will stay tasty for up to a month.

Makes 4–8 popsicles

3 egg yolks
80g honey – the best quality you can find
200ml double cream

Place the yolks in the bowl of an electric mixer with a whisk attachment, set the speed on maximum and leave it running so that they start to foam up.

While the yolks are whisking, heat the honey in a small pan until it reaches the boil (you can heat it for 2–3 minutes in the microwave if you prefer), then remove from the heat. Very carefully pour the hot honey in a slow constant drizzle into the yolks and continue whisking until the mix is really fluffy and shiny.

Lightly whip the cream. It is very important to keep it soft: the whipped cream should just reach the 'soft ribbon' stage where it starts to hold its shape. If in doubt, for this dessert it is better to under-whip than over-whip. Fold the honey-egg mixture into the whipped cream, then use to fill the moulds. Place a lolly stick in the centre of each one and freeze for at least 4 hours or until you are ready to be a child again.

White chocolate, pine nuts, olive oil & candied lemon zest

We generally see no point in white chocolate – it is good for nothing except this wonderful dessert, where it works with the olive oil to create silk-on-silk smoothness, while the lemon and pine nuts bring interesting accents. At the restaurant we use a delicious Greek olive oil, its bitter finish works beautifully with the rich cream. That bottle of olive oil you bought for the price of a laptop when you got drunk at the River Café will come in handy here...

Makes 4 portions – it may not look like much but it is very rich, so you don't need a lot

200ml double cream
100g white chocolate
1 tbsp olive oil, plus 1 tbsp to finish
1 lemon
enough water to cover x 2, plus 50ml
50g sugar
40g pine nuts, roasted till golden (see method on page 10)
4 tiny pinches of sea salt, to finish

Heat the cream in a pan over a high heat until it is boiling, then pour over the white chocolate in a bowl. Add 1 tablespoon of olive oil and whisk in circular motions to combine (whisking in one direction only, so that you don't break the texture), until the chocolate has melted. Cover and place in the fridge to cool for at least for 6 hours or overnight.

Peel strips of the lemon skin (just the yellow part, without any white pith) and cut into very thin slices – you can use a special long zester for this, if you own one, but it is just as easy to do with a peeler and a sharp knife. Place the zest strips in a small pan, cover with water and bring to the boil over a high heat. Drain, re-cover with water and bring to the boil again. Drain for a second time (by now all the bitterness should be gone) and cover with 50ml of fresh water. Add the sugar and return to the boil, then reduce the heat to low and simmer for 5 minutes. Remove from the heat and allow to cool.

When you are ready to serve, whisk the white chocolate cream until it thickens and starts to hold its shape, but don't over-whip – the fat content is so high, you may end up with butter instead. Carefully spoon into your loveliest glasses. Top each one with some pine nuts, a pinch of sea salt, a touch of olive oil and some candied lemon zest.

Chocolate, cardamom & bitter orange

We got an email from a girl asking for work in our kitchen, signed Georgia Middleton. Our email back said – are you the third Middleton sister? When can you come? She arrived wearing oversized glasses, neon-coloured trainers and a cape made of Astro-turf, looking more like Harry Potter's sister than Kate and Pippa's. We changed her name to Pippa anyway and gave her a job. She hoped to do pastry but ended up kitchen, and is doing a terrific job there, but she still has a soft spot for sweet things and squeaks when we make canapé desserts for parties (she's a squeaker).

This dessert is perfect in a little cup as a bit of it goes a long way; the orange, cardamom and sea salt make it a very sophisticated, grown-up affair.

4 generous portions

For the mousse
150g dark chocolate (choose your favourite)
75g butter
1 tsp ground cardamom pods (page 11)
3 eggs
100g soft dark brown sugar
sea salt, to finish

For the bitter orange syrup
60g sugar
1 orange, zest and juice
50ml water

Melt the chocolate and butter with the cardamom in a glass or Pyrex bowl set over a pan of boiling water. Whip the eggs and sugar together with a whisk in a separate bowl until foamy, pale and thick. Fold in the melted chocolate mixture and stir until combined. Cover and place in the fridge to cool for at least 2 hours.

Heat the sugar for the syrup in a small pan on a high heat and stir until you have a dark caramel. Add the orange zest, juice and water to the pan – be careful, as it will spit and the sugar will clump – and reduce the heat to low. Continue cooking and stirring slowly until the sugar is completely dissolved. Remove from the heat and allow to cool a little before serving.

Serve a spoonful of the chocolate cream per person and drizzle with the syrup. Finish with some sea salt and a large dollop of sour cream or crème fraiche if you want.

Yogurt mousse with cherry and pomegranate granita

This is a happy marriage of two perfect summer desserts – the light and tangy yogurt mousse just needs a bit of fruit to complete it; the granita made with the last of the cherries and the first of the pomegranates is refreshing and flavourful enough to have on its own. Together they are a beautiful-looking and delicious dessert, and exactly what you want on a hot day. We use *mahleb* in this recipe, a bittersweet spice that complements the flavours so well; replace it with vanilla if you can't get hold of any *mahleb*. For the best results use a strained yogurt – you can either buy it ready-strained (like Total Greek yogurt) or hang 500g of natural yogurt in some cheesecloth over a bowl for 2 hours to yield 300g of strained. Make sure to start the granita at least a day in advance as it takes time to freeze, but once made it will keep in the freezer for 2 weeks.

Makes 4–6

For the cherry and pomegranate granita
2 pomegranates
250g cherries
2 tbsp sugar
2 tbsp boiling water
juice of ½ lemon (1 tbsp)
juice of ½ orange (2 tbsp)

For the mousse
2 egg whites
60g honey
300g strained yogurt
1 tsp ground mahleb

Crack one of the pomegranates open and remove 3–4 tablespoons of the seeds to serve with the finished dessert later on. Squeeze the juice out of the remainder of that pomegranate and the whole one; this is very easy – use a citrus press, or a home juicer or just press the pomegranates until all the little seeds explode and let out their juice.

Reserve about 12–14 cherries to use as garnish and stone the rest. Purée the stoned cherries with the pomegranate juice, sugar, water, lemon juice and orange juice. Strain through a fine sieve into a bowl or plastic container and place in the freezer. Give the mixture an hour to start to freeze, then use a fork to smash it up. Return to the freezer and repeat 3–4 times until the juice is all frozen into lovely crystals.

Now for the mousse. Place the egg whites in a mixer bowl with a whisk attachment and whisk until they start to go white and fluffy. Heat the honey in a small pan till it boils, then pour into the whites in a steady drizzle. Continue whisking until the mixture forms a strong shiny meringue.

In a separate bowl mix the yogurt and *mahleb*. Take a spoonful of the meringue and stir through to release the yogurt a little, then carefully fold the rest of the meringue into the yogurt. Spoon into a glass serving bowl, or individual dishes or glasses, and chill the mousse until ready to serve.

To serve, scoop the granita onto the yogurt mousse and decorate with the reserved cherries and pomegranate seeds.

Cherry, pistachio & coconut cake

This was the first cake I made for the restaurant. We wanted something that would sit on the bar counter and just make people stare. It has been with us from the first day and I have a feeling it will stay there until the end. We do vary the fruit on top, so we use red plums or yellow plums or raspberries, but really the cherries are the best version. The contrast between the cherries and the green pistachios, and the addition of *mahleb* to the cake batter, together create something electric. It is such an easy recipe to follow, I am sure it will become a huge favourite in any household.

Makes a 22cm diameter ring cake

100g sugar, plus 20g for the topping
90g light brown sugar
180g ground almonds
30g ground pistachios
45g desiccated coconut
50g self-raising flour
a pinch of salt
1 tsp ground mahleb
150g butter, melted
3 eggs
300g cherries
50g roughly chopped pistachios,
   for the topping

Preheat the oven to 190°C/170°C fan/ gas mark 5 and lightly grease a 22cm diameter ring cake tin with butter.

Mix all the dry ingredients together in a large bowl. Pour over the melted butter and mix in the eggs. Spoon the batter into the pre-greased tin and smooth down.

Remove the stones from the cherries – you can do this with a cherry stoner or by just pulling them apart and popping the stones out with your fingers. I like to do this over the cake tin, so that any juice drips onto the cake and adds colour. Drop the pitted cherries onto the batter and sprinkle the top of the cake with the remaining 20g of sugar and the roughly chopped pistachios. Bake for 25–30 minutes until the cake between the cherries goes all golden.

Allow the cake to cool in the tin, as it needs time to settle, then gently remove by running a knife around the edges. Covered well, it will keep in the fridge for up to a week (not much chance of that happening), but for the best flavour, allow it to return to room temperature before eating.

Marzipan cookies

Mathew and Rebecca live a few doors down on Warren Street and adopted us from the day we opened. We are always on a mission to plump up skinny Mathew, who does not put on an ounce, even though he comes in almost every day to have cake for elevenses. And we always make sure to have a few gluten-free things for Rebecca, who single-handedly made these cookies a hit.

Makes 9 large or 18 small cookies

150g marzipan (best to use a high almond content one – around 60%)
2 egg whites
100g ground almonds
50g icing sugar
zest of ½ orange
1 tsp sweet spice mix (page 12)
100–150g flaked or nibbed almonds, to coat

Break the marzipan into small pieces in a large bowl and beat in the egg whites until it forms a smooth paste. Add the ground almonds, icing sugar, zest and spice and mix well to combine. Cover and chill overnight.

Preheat the oven to 190°C/170°C fan/gas mark 5.

Place the flaked or nibbed almonds in a wide bowl. You'll need two spoons for the next stage. Scoop up a big spoonful of the chilled cookie mix with one spoon and push it off into the flaked almonds with the other. Roll the spoonful of mixture around to coat it all over, then carefully pick it up and place on a baking sheet. Press down to flatten slightly. Leave some space between the cookies, as they do spread a little when baking. You can freeze them on the sheet at this stage, to bake at a later time (just bring them back up to room temperature before baking).

Bake in the centre of the oven for 10 minutes, then turn the tray around and bake for 5–8 minutes more, until the cookies are a light golden colour but still soft to the touch. Allow to cool on the tray. These will keep well in an airtight container for 4–5 days.

My version of a maamool cookie

Traditional *maamool* cookies are usually filled with dates or walnuts and making them is very labour-intensive. It is all about the lovely patterns created by tiny pincers, which takes much practice. I have never really had the time to learn to make these patterns (I still hope a granny somewhere will take me in and teach me her art), so I have settled for a version which is simpler-looking but no less fantastic to eat. If you do end up in a market in the Middle East and see loads of little flat pincers in a basket, buy a pair and practise pinching the dough, then maybe one day you can teach me.

Makes 12–14 cookies

For the pastry
120g margarine or other vegetable fat
    spread (I know it is frowned upon, but
    really it works better than butter
    in these)
125g plain flour
85g semolina
2 tbsp icing sugar
a pinch of salt
1 tbsp orange blossom water
about 60ml warm water

For the filling
50g golden raisins
50g roasted pistachios, roughly chopped
2 tbsp good quality honey
½ tsp ground cinnamon
½ tsp ground cardamom pods (page 11)

Put the raisins in a bowl and pour enough boiling water over to cover them. Leave to soak for 25–30 minutes, then drain them and combine with the other filling ingredients to form a thick mass.

Cube the margarine and rub into the flour, semolina, icing sugar and salt. Add the orange blossom water and just enough of the warm water to bring it to a lovely, smooth pastry dough. Cover with cling film and allow to rest for half an hour in a cool place, but don't refrigerate it.

Preheat your oven to 190°C/170°C fan/gas mark 5.

Divide the pastry into twelve pieces of about 30g and roll each into a ball. Flatten a ball on your palm until it covers it and is quite thin, then blob a teaspoonful of the filling in the centre. Fold the pastry over the filling to seal it in, roll it back into the shape of a ball and set on a baking tray. (This would be the time to make the lovely patterns with pincers or a *maamool* cookie mould, or just use a fork.)

Once all your cookies are filled, bake them in the centre of the oven until the pastry starts to turn golden. This will take about 10–15 minutes. Allow to cool on a wire rack before serving – just as they are, or dusted with icing sugar if you fancy it. These will keep well in an airtight container for 4–5 days.

Drinks.

'Look at the elder trees,' I said to Itamar. 'They are just starting to blossom. I can't wait until we can start picking.'

He looked back at me. 'You know what this means?'

'Of course I do. It means we get elderflower cordial back on the menu, my absolute favourite drink of all time.'

'Yes that, but also do you realise this means it has been a year?'

I paused. It had. A whole year in our little restaurant had just passed by. It had somehow felt like both the shortest year of our lives and the longest.

We opened in June 2012. The elderflowers were just coming into bloom and we picked some. We ended up making five litres of cordial, thinking it would last us the entire year. We had run out by the end of August. Then in early autumn we roasted plums and vanilla for a dessert and started making iced tea from the syrup. In winter we changed to quince and cinnamon; in spring strawberry and rose; and now we had come full circle, as the elderflowers were out again.

This year, 2013, we wrote our first cookbook, and in June we made 80 litres of elderflower cordial. By August there were just five left. We can only imagine what next year will bring.

It has been a year full of surprises, excitement, heartbreak and great happiness. For me the most amazing moment was when we left the kitchen in the hands of our dedicated staff and walked away for our first evening out with friends. We had faith that whatever happened at the restaurant, it would be OK and our staff would survive. Like parents leaving their kids with the babysitter for the first time, we checked our phones every hour. The only message was a tweet from a regular saying that dinner was great, as ever.

Itamar amazed me too. He had never worked on a restaurant floor – no one in their right mind would believe he could: big, clumsy, messy, always bumping into things, breaking glasses, spilling drinks – but he was, and is, brilliant at it. Not to say that he doesn't still do all those things, but he brings life and joy to the room and he loves people. He loves seeing them happy, having a chat, eating, going through life's celebrations and dramas. I hide downstairs in the kitchen most of the time. I listen to people laughing at his jokes, and sometimes to the sound of crashing glass (at which point sweet Danielle knows that's his cue to grab the dustpan and brush). Occasionally I will pop upstairs, and even I know some of the people by name and face: Tony, James, Miki and Meital, Fran, Jo, Andrew and Rose, blue-eyed Roberta, David Gilmore, and many others. They are more than just customers to us.

A community has happened. Who would have thought it? Here in central London, on a little side street that ends in a hospital, there exists a microcosm of the world. It is our version of the world, where food, drink, our customers and our employees (and we two) are all equally important to the tiny ecosystem. We love it, but it is also the scariest experience. We have put ourselves out there, on the street, our door open to all, friend or foe. In the world of restaurants, people may love you or hate you; they may write wonderful emails and reviews; or for whatever reason they may have a dreadful time and slate you in public. For us it is always personal and we feel it all – we laugh, we rejoice, we cringe, we cry, we try harder, and sometimes we get it just right. Hopefully we do this time, in this book, too.

Cold drinks

Most of the recipes in this chapter involve a base sugar syrup. I've set out the recipe for it below, but you can always just dissolve sugar in hot water (using a 1g:1ml sugar-water ratio) and use that instead. You may want to adjust the amount of sweetness slightly in each case to suit personal taste. These recipes will make 4–6 glasses, depending on the size of glass. We store our teas in the fridge in old (thoroughly washed) milk bottles, and all but the jasmine and green melon iced tea will keep well for 3–4 days.

Base sugar syrup

200g sugar
200ml water
1 tbsp glucose or honey

Mix everything together in a small pan and bring to the boil over a high heat, then reduce the heat and simmer for 2 minutes. Leave to cool, then transfer to a clean bottle or other container and store in your fridge for up to a week.

Orange blossom iced tea

We always have this on the menu and probably always will. As chefs from a hot country working in hot kitchens, we have developed a palate for thirst-quenchers, and this one is up there with the best of them. We have been asked for the recipe so many times, but until now had obliged only once. As a result, we know for a fact that this has been prepared and enjoyed in Dubai as part of an *Iftoor* meal, the Ramadan fast-breaking dinner at the end of the day.

1.5 litres water
2 Earl Grey tea bags
300ml base sugar syrup (page 266)
2 tsp orange blossom water
4 sprigs of fresh mint
1 orange, cut in thin slices, skin and all

To pimp (optional)
  fresh mint leaves
  1–2 shots of rum per person

Bring the water to the boil in a pan, add the tea bags and stir around. Turn off the heat and leave to steep for 15 minutes.

Remove the tea bags, add the sugar syrup and orange blossom water, and stir to mix. Decant into a bottle or jug and push in the mint sprigs and orange slices. Place in the fridge to cool entirely. Serve with loads of ice.

To pimp your tea, crush some fresh mint leaves at the bottom of a lowball glass, add a shot or two of rum, then top up with the iced tea and lots of ice.

Lemonade

If life gives you lemons, consider yourself lucky – we love lemonade. Our favourite is the one Margaret Tayar in Jaffa makes. She cooks the entire lemon and blends the fruit to a pulp with sugar. Then when a table orders a jug of lemonade, she just adds water and plenty of ice – delish. Others put loads of mint in it, until it resembles mouthwash rather than a drink. We go light: base sugar syrup with freshly-squeezed lemon juice (Pierre Paolo, our miniature kitchen porter, spends an hour every morning juicing lemons and oranges) and sprigs of fresh mint. We use a standard ratio but always taste to adjust, as the lemons vary in acidity and sweetness.

250ml fresh lemon juice (about 5–6 lemons)
150ml base sugar syrup (page 266)
600ml water
4 sprigs of fresh mint

To pimp (optional)
  vodka

Mix all the ingredients together in a jug, then sample and adjust to taste. Serve over loads of ice.

Pimp it with vodka, of course – as much as you can take.

Elderflower cordial

Bridget, a.k.a. 'Daughter of Phil', is a dear friend. Apart from helping us move flats when she was 8 months pregnant, doing DIY for us when we are too busy to fix a shelf, stamping Honey & Co bags, baking my birthday cakes (because no one else will dare), waiting for a repair man to fix our boiler, opening the door to our flat for family who come to visit when we are just too busy and many more little things that save us on a daily basis, she is also in charge of our elderflower foraging. She grabs her daughters, a few bags and a pair of scissors and heads into London parks to forage elderflowers in bloom. It's a short season in early June, and last year we could not make enough of this amazing cordial. True, it isn't Middle Eastern at all – in fact we only got to know these beautiful blooms when we moved to the UK – but just as now Bridget has finally joined Honey & Co in an official capacity as pastry chef (not just friend and forager), so can elderflower join the traditional Middle Eastern array of cold beverages.

1.2 litres water
1kg sugar
3 lemons, halved
20g citric acid (lemon salt)
10–15 heads of elderflower blossom

To pimp (optional)
1–2 shots of sloe gin per person
sparkling water

Boil the water, sugar and lemons
together in a large pan over a high heat for 5 minutes. Use a pair of tongs to squeeze out any remaining juice from the lemons and discard, then stir in the citric acid. Allow to cool a little (for about 10 minutes), then add the blossoms, cover and leave to steep at room temperature overnight. Strain through a very fine sieve into a bottle or other container and store in the fridge. Dilute to taste with water to serve.

You can keep the cordial in the fridge for up to a month. If you want to keep it for longer, you will need to seal it in sterilised bottles while it is hot.

To pimp your cordial, pour a shot or two of sloe gin into a highball glass, add a tablespoon or two of cordial, and top up with ice and sparkling water. Stir, drink, repeat.

Roasted strawberry & rose iced tea (for spring)

You will need access to unsprayed fresh roses for this. If you have none growing in the garden and no friends who can provide you with rose petals, you'll have to loot neighbouring gardens at night. If you live near Brixton Academy and wake up one day to find your roses missing, we had nothing to do with it, honest. If you really can't get hold of rose petals, rose water will do.

200g strawberries, halved and
    stalks removed
100g sugar
1.5 litres water
1 tbsp dried mint (or 2 mint tea bags)
a handful of fresh rose petals
    (or 1–2 tsp rose water)

To pimp (optional)
    1–2 shots of vodka per person
    fresh mint leaves
    fresh strawberries, sliced

Preheat the oven to 220°C/200°C fan/ gas mark 7. Mix the strawberries and sugar in a roasting tin and roast in the centre of the oven for 5 minutes.

Bring the water to the boil in a pan, add the dried mint and rose petals and stir around. Turn off the heat and leave to infuse for 15 minutes. If you are using rose water rather than rose petals, add the first teaspoon and taste to see whether you want to add another. Some people prefer it less perfumed than others.

Add the roasted strawberries and leave to infuse again, this time for 10 minutes. Strain and decant into a serving jug, then chill in the fridge. Serve with loads of ice.

To pimp your tea, put a shot or two of vodka, a load of mint leaves and some fresh strawberry slices in each glass, and top up with the iced tea and plenty of ice.

Jasmine & green melon iced tea (for summer)

Sweet jasmine is the symbol of summertime for me – bushes of it growing every-where in Jerusalem, its delicate white flowers scenting the streets on hot summer nights. This is not a tea that keeps well, as you don't cook the melon at all; however, the result is extremely fresh and lively. Perfect for a hot summer's day.

1.5 litres water
2 jasmine green tea bags
½ green Galia melon (the one with the
* rough skin)*
200g base sugar syrup (page 266)
4–6 sprigs of lemon thyme or verbena,
* to serve*

To pimp (optional)
* lemon thyme or verbena*
* 2 shots of Midori melon liqueur (or 1 shot of*
*   Midori and 1 shot of vodka) per person*

Bring the water to the boil in a pan, add the tea bags and stir around. Turn off the heat and leave to steep and cool for 15 minutes.

Peel and cube the melon. Place it in a blender or food processor with the sugar syrup and blitz until smooth. Remove the tea bags from the cooled tea and mix in the sweetened melon purée. Transfer to a jug and chill for an hour, or serve with masses of ice.

If you can get your hands on a little lemon thyme or lemon verbena, pop a sprig in each glass with loads of ice before pouring in the iced tea.

To pimp your tea, muddle some lemon thyme or verbena in a highball glass, add the Midori (or Midori and vodka), and top up with the iced tea and lots of ice.

Plum & vanilla iced tea (for autumn)

This excellent tea, like many good things, was born of a mistake. One day, when roasting plums to serve with marzipan cake, a certain Italian pastry chef forgot them in the oven for far too long. I hate wastage, especially of amazing plums and vanilla, so I came up with this iced tea. It is truthfully worth overcooking plums for.

6–8 soft red plums (about 400g)
1 vanilla pod
200g sugar
1.5 litres water
1 jasmine green tea bag

To pimp (optional)
  1–2 shots of gin per person
  fresh lemon slices

Preheat the oven to 220°C/200°C fan/ gas mark 7.

Cut each plum into 6–8 wedges, discarding the stone, and place in a roasting tin. Slit the vanilla pod all the way down its length and scrape the seeds out (I use the back of the knife that I slit it with). Put the seeds and the pod on the plum wedges and sprinkle everything with the sugar.

Place the roasting tin in the top of the oven for 12–14 minutes, after which there should be a bright red liquid forming around the plums. If it hasn't appeared yet, return them to the oven for another 5–6 minutes. Don't worry if the plums lose their shape.

While the plums are roasting, bring the water to the boil in a pan, add the tea bag and stir around, then remove from the heat.

Once the plums are cooked, pour the tea over them and mix to combine and dissolve any sugar residue. Allow to infuse for 10 minutes, then strain into a serving jug. Serve with loads of ice.

To pimp your tea, serve with buckets of gin and plenty of ice, and a bit of fresh lemon.

Quince & cinnamon iced tea (for winter)

This is a by-product of our constant quince poaching. The liquid that remains is so laden with wonderful quince flavour, it's a shame to let it go to waste. Make this when you're preparing poached quince with curd cheese and honeyed hazelnuts (page 134) or if you decide to poach quince to serve with marzipan and almond cakes (page 244).

2 quinces
1 litre + 500ml water
juice of 2 lemons
400g sugar
1 cinnamon stick
2 English Breakfast tea bags

To pimp (optional)
  1–2 shots of brandy per person
  honey
  cayenne pepper

Cut each quince into 8–10 wedges and remove the core and the seeds. I keep the skin on but you can peel them if you prefer. Place the quince wedges in a pan, cover with a litre of water and add the lemon juice, sugar and cinnamon stick. Bring to the boil and cook for 10 minutes on a medium heat. Remove the pan from the heat, but leave the quinces in the liquid to continue cooking and infusing as they cool. You can store them for up to a week in their poaching liquid in an airtight container in the fridge.

Bring the remaining 500ml of water to the boil in a pan, add the tea bags and stir around, then remove from the heat and leave to infuse for 15 minutes.

Strain the quince cooking liquor (setting the fruit aside to use in other recipes) and add to the tea infusion. Transfer to a jug and chill for an hour, or serve with masses of ice.

To pimp your tea, pour a single or double shot of brandy into a lowball glass and add a bit of honey and a bit of cayenne. Stir well and top up with the iced tea and loads of ice.

Hot drinks

I never see the point of hot tea, for me. It is just low-rent, poor man's coffee, and as much as I love my adoptive country and try to embrace its customs, it is not something I can bring myself to like. Except when my wife makes it. She has a sixth sense for just the right brewing time, amount of sugar, temperature and cup. She rarely makes herself tea these days, at least not when I'm around, knowing she will get to drink very little of it. These two infusions are her idea, and though they aren't my cup of tea (excuse the pun, you know I had to...), they have quite a fan base amongst our customers.

Hot cinnamon & rose infusion

For a 4-cup teapot

2 cinnamon sticks
2 heaped tbsp dried rose petals or the petals
of 3 fresh roses from your garden
600ml boiling water

Break the cinnamon stick a little and place with the rose petals in the teapot. Pour the boiling water over and let it infuse for 5 minutes before serving.

Persian lemon & fennel infusion

For a 4-cup teapot

4 whole dried Persian lemons
2 heaped tbsp whole fennel seeds
3 thick slices of fresh lemon
600ml boiling water

Cut the dried lemons in half (or crush them) and mix with the fennel seeds and fresh lemon slices in the teapot. Pour the boiling water over and let it infuse for 5 minutes before serving.

Mint tea

Fresh herb infusions are very common where we come from. You can use sage to great effect; sweet geranium and savory can both make a good drink, as does lemon verbena; but the best, and the most common, is fresh mint infusion. The method is similar for all these herbs and very simple – fill the teapot with loads and loads of fresh mint (or verbena or whatever), more than you think you need, then top up with boiling water and leave to infuse for a minute or so. Smelling this is as good as drinking it.

Turkish coffee

We love drinking Turkish coffee and it was obvious to us that we were going to serve it at Honey & Co. We sourced our little copper coffee pots and got four kilos of our favourite coffee from an Arab village in Israel, and thought to ourselves we would never get through it all as no one would buy it. Two weeks later I was calling my brother to bring me more coffee on his next visit, and now every guest who is willing to courier for us ends up carrying bags of coffee from Israel in his or her luggage. We cook this coffee to order in the kitchen. If we get an order towards the tail end of lunch service, we may make a bigger pot – some for the order, some for us, and some for Rachael, who prefers it to pretty much anything.

Add 1 teaspoon of freshly ground cardamom pods for every 250g of Turkish coffee – you can keep this mixture in an airtight bag or other container in the fridge. Use 1 heaped tablespoon of the mixture (and 1 cup of water) for every cup of coffee.

Put the coffee and cardamom together with the water in a small saucepan and slowly bring to the boil over a medium heat, stirring so that all the coffee grounds infuse. Once it has come to the boil, remove from the heat, skim the first foam formed, then add a teaspoon of sugar for each cup that you are making. Return the mixture to the boil. Remove from the heat again, stir and then return to the boil for the final time. Pour into the cups and allow the coffee grounds to settle before drinking. Make sure not to drink them by mistake – they are horrible.

Publishers and authors hardly ever get the chance to have a relationship like we have – as soon as we opened our restaurant across the road from Hodder's offices, you took us under your wings. We now proudly see ourselves as the 'Hodder canteen'. The support we got from you both as our publishers and as individual customers is invaluable. So many of you are entwined in our day to day:
Sue trying the first desserts from the kitchen, Roland's postcard bookings, Martin Nield's perfectly imperfect quince and Jo's morning milk bun. We thank you all and will miss you so once you move.

Together we would like to thank:
Elizabeth Hallett for her patience, grace and wisdom and for putting up with the noisy Israeli couple invading her life, Alice Laurent for ignoring us time and again and making better decisions than we can, and Patricia 'the red mullet' Niven, who understood us from the first minute and knew what we wanted, then took it up a notch and made it so much more – you are all geniuses. Thanks also to Clare for her shitty music and great collages, to Jason, the imaginary assistant, to Kate for connecting the dots, to Cynthia for propping and to Rosie Gailer, for always taking such good care of this book and us. A special thank you in an airtight container to Bryony (aka Brian E) – it will keep for up to a week in the fridge. Also to the ringmaster Luigi and Ajda the tiger for arranging the most spectacular circus for us and to all the publishers who were kind enough to meet us.

To all of our staff, past and present, you're a terrific bunch. A lot of you appear in these pages, so will not be repeated here, but we would like to mention Asia, Begona, Kamila, Katie, Sabrina, Hussain (aka Juice) and Kate, who joined after most stories were written and never got a story of their own – hopefully next time. We are lucky to have you. Wielkie dzięki to Andy Wojcik without whom not a single plate of food would ever leave our kitchen.

Then to our friends and inspirations: Ill-illshemesh, who came to help us at the right time, Shachar for never losing his appetite for us and our food, Jaap for cooking so many of these recipes and sending notes and picture proof. Sami, Yotam, Noam and Cornelia for friendship and advice. Erez and Yonit, Inbal and Ben, Oshrat and Gal, Savarna, Mark, Amit, Nikki, Liat, Nirit, Charissa and Basia, your friendship and help is invaluable.

From Itamar – To my mother for her love. To my brother, my hero, for not giving up on me. To Dani Regev for his onion rice and much else. Eynav Berman, Orna Agmon and Ella Shine, the unacknowledged godmothers of Honey & Co, there is a trace of you in everything I do. Miri, Ben and Ishai: I talk to you all in my head every day, your voices always with me, even if I don't pick up the phone. To my wife, who is everything I want: never has anyone been so lucky in love, or better served by it.

From Sarit – To my mum and dad for letting me do my thing (even though they would have preferred a university degree first) and to my sister and brother and their amazing families for eating all my food, for sending me pictures and messages and for (kind of) forgiving me for moving away. To my husband, who has challenged me to do things I would have never attempted without his support and energy, and especially for showing me that love, fun and work can all fit into one life without making compromises.

A big thank you to every single customer who ever came and an extra thanks to those who came back – please don't stop. We thank everyone who enjoyed Honey & Co and told someone about it and for the truly lovely reviews from the *Time Out London* team, Marina O'Loughlin, Nick Lander, Grace Dent, Zoe Williams, Xanthe Clay, Adrian Gill, Jay Rayner, Alan Jenkins and the entire *Observer* team, and every blog post, tweet and review.

Index

First published in Great Britain in 2014 by Saltyard Books
An imprint of Hodder & Stoughton
An Hachette UK company

1

Copyright © Saritamar Media Limited 2014
Photography © Patricia Niven 2014

The right of Saritamar Media Limited to be identified as the Author of the Work has been asserted by them in accordance with the Copyright, Designs and Patents Act 1988.

A CIP catalogue record for this title is available from the British Library.

ISBN 978 1 444 75467 4
eBook ISBN 978 1 444 75468 1

'I got hunger' on page v is taken from the song 'Got The Hunger?' from the album *Pot Of Gold*. Written by Alice Russell & Alex Cowan. Appears courtesy of 5MM Publishing.

Book design by Aka Alice
Typeset in Miller, Capita and Bohemian Typewriter

Copy editor Bryony Nowell
Proof reader Annie Lee
Indexer Hilary Bird
Photography assistant Clare Lewington

Printed and bound in Germany by Mohn Media

Hodder & Stoughton policy is to use papers that are natural, renewable and recyclable products and made from wood grown in sustainable forests. The logging and manufacturing processes are expected to conform to the environmental regulations of the country of origin.

Saltyard Books
338 Euston Road
London NW1 3BH

www.saltyardbooks.co.uk